A GUIDEBOOK FOR THE SPIRITUAL LIFE

Bernard Peyrous

A Guidebook for the Spiritual Life

HOW SHOULD ONE LIVE WITH GOD?

Translated by
Myles Rearden CM

the columba press

First published in 2006 by
the columba press
55A Spruce Avenue, Stillorgan Industrial Park,
Blackrock, Co Dublin
in association with
Editions de l'Emmanuel, Paris

Cover by Bill Bolger
Origination by The Columba Press
Printed in Ireland

ISBN 1 85607 535 4

Acknowledgements

Quotations from the psalms are taken either from the Grail version or J. Rhymer's translation in *The Psalms*, St Paul's, Slough, 1994. Quotations from St Teresa of Avila are taken from E. Allison Peers' translation in *St Teresa's Complete Works*, 3 vols, Sheed and Ward, London and New York, 1946.

Copyright © 2006, Bernard Peyrous

Table of Contents

Translator's Preface		7
Introduction		9

PART ONE: THE FOUNDATIONS OF LIFE WITH GOD

1:	Why and How God acts	16
2:	How can people respond?	33

PART TWO: THE STAGES OF THE SPIRITUAL LIFE

3:	The Beginnings of the Spiritual Life	58
4:	Progressing in the Spiritual Life	77
5:	Life of union with God	101

PART THREE:
TOWARDS A BETTER UNDERSTANDING OF THE SPIRITUAL LIFE

6:	The variety of spiritual itineraries and the personal call	120
7:	The Different Spiritualities	131
8:	The 'Second Call'	145
9:	Woundedness and spiritual life	163
10:	Extraordinary events in the spiritual life	176

Conclusion	194
Notes	196

Translator's Preface

Bernard Peyrous attracted my attention with a preface he wrote to a study of St Vincent de Paul.[1] A visit to the internet led me to what was then his latest book, which is that translated here. I sent away for it, and on reading it became convinced that here was exactly what a good many people had been waiting for: a clear, well thought-out and reader-friendly guidebook to the spiritual life. Fr Peyrous kindly accepted my offer to translate his book, and The Columba Press shared my view of its potential enough to undertake its publication.

A Guidebook to the Spiritual Life is well suited to our time. The men and women whose lives it grew out of include, among others, a film critic, a prisoner of war, teachers, students, business people, agriculturalists, carers of the handicapped and parents, as well as religious sisters and brothers, and priests. Many of them are our contemporaries. But the book can still present people and writings from the past, especially the scriptures, without losing its relevance. Fr Peyrous has something of Pope Benedict's skill at showing how much Christianity is at home in the setting of today.

There are three parts in the book. The first lays down the basis for the spiritual adventure: the reality of God and his commitment to the happiness of the human race. The second sets out the stages that anyone will pass through as their spiritual life unfolds, though in a uniquely personal way for each one. And the third examines in greater detail how this has happened in the lives of some individuals, some of the spiritual movements that have emerged and are continuing at the present time, how there can be a new beginning in mid-life, how even the greatest seeming disasters are no obstacles to the spiritual life, and what kinds of divine interaction anyone can expect to experience.

The most notable feature of Fr Peyrous's book is his use of the *Interior Castle* of St Teresa of Avila. He is convinced that her

---

1. G.Toscani, *The Spirituality of the Poor (La mystique des Pauvres)*,Ed. Saint Paul, Versailles, 1998.

account of passing through seven 'dwelling places' on the way to God is the most helpful schema on offer: that is a view I have long shared. Naturally, it needs to be understood carefully. The spiritual life is not an actual journey or the exploration of a building. Spirituality is the relation between a human being and God, a personal relationship. There is no single schema that exactly fits everyone's relationship with God. But it is helpful to have it clearly stated that the spiritual life involves growing, experiencing difficulties and ultimately enjoying a union with God within this life. The schema also raises the question, though it does not answer it, of which 'dwelling place' is appropriate for, say, admission into a training programme for ordination, or for an ordained minister in any church. Interestingly, Fr Peyrous indicates once or twice that readers of his book will be some way into the 'dwelling places'.

For the purposes of an English-speaking readership, and with the generous approval of the author, there have been two alterations to the text of the book, both of them in the third part. I have written a short section entitled 'Spirituality for Lay People: St Francis de Sales and his Movement' to replace one dealing with the French School of Spirituality (chapter 7), and a section dealing with Marie de la Trinité has been omitted altogether (chapter 6). Also, two of the short biographical passages in chapter 6 have been considerably re-written to make their contexts clearer. Finally, I have occasionally added notes outside the text to clarify some points: they are marked *Tr*. Otherwise everything remains as close as possible to the warm and attractive writing of Fr Bernard Peyrous, who is a Catholic priest of the diocese of Bordeaux, and belongs to the Emmanuel Community. To him, and to Seán O Boyle of The Columba Press for his editorial skill, I express my deep gratitude.

Myles Rearden CM
St Patrick's College
Maynooth
18 February 2006

Introduction

The most important thing in life
Is there any one thing in life that is more important than everything else, that gives it meaning, value and fragrance? There is. It is one's relationship with God, bringing with it a new relationship with other people. By this I mean the deep relationship which affects our whole being, under the guidance of the soul. Living with God is what produces joy and well-being in life. 'The life of a human being is the vision of God', as St Irenaeus rightly says.

If you are convinced of that, this book is for you. It is for you if you want to set out on the great adventure of the relationship with God. It is also for you if you have already encountered God in a real way, and at least started on the journey with him. And it is for you if you have been living with him for years. If you want to advance further in life with God, perhaps this book will help you.

Why? The life with God is fascinating, but it is not always obvious. It has its periods of light and of darkness. It has a pleasant side, and also a disconcerting side. It is not always clear how one is getting on, or what to do. There can be wrong turnings. St Teresa of Avila says a great deal in her books about the diversions and blockages she met at various times of her life. My experience is that one makes better progress with a little help from others. Anyone who has travelled at all has found a guidebook useful. What is offered here, things being as they are, is a sort of guidebook or itinerary for the spiritual life.

Are there not plenty of guidebooks already for the spiritual life? There certainly are many accounts of how to live with God. So why write another?

Why this book?
There is a whole literature on the life with God. However, my

experience is that there is a certain lack in this area at present. Let me explain.

I was forty when I was ordained a priest. Before that, I was a research historian. I thought that my studies and my experience in compiling detailed accounts of personal lives provided me with a certain understanding of life. My area of specialisation was the history of spirituality, which I thought gave me some ideas on how God deals with people in order to lead them to himself. I was very familiar with the literature, especially biographies. That was all to the good, but in reality I knew hardly anything.

At the end of a year in the priesthood, I realised just how little I knew. There were many things about the human soul and the ways of God of which I was ignorant. As a priest, I had the joy of hearing many confessions. I had heard it all! And I also had the joy of coming to know many people in a very deep way. It was a blessing to have listened to so many people. Many were converts, others had lived their faith since childhood. Some were certainly saints, and others came to be considered saints after their death. I had also helped people who were dying, and given some retreats. These are circumstances when one goes to the roots of human life and comes to know what people are really like.

Associating closely with souls, with people, has genuinely been the joy of my life. Of course, the cross was also part of it. But out of the double phenomena of happiness and suffering I have seen a great deal of good emerge. Not only for the people involved, but for human society in general and for the whole church: 'The church is born in souls', as the German theologian Romano Guardini says. To put it differently, 'tomorrow's society is born in the consciences of today'. And God is present in that.

I now know that one who accompanies souls requires experience more than anything else. But I also know that there are necessary stages along the way, conversions that must take place for everyone, and phenomena that occur frequently. I have read a great deal, but I have often felt that I would like to have a practical book to explain things clearly. One has to get one's thoughts in order. One remarkable man of the spirit, Fr Jerome of the abbey of Sept-Fons, wrote to me: 'Whether one likes it or not, the union of human beings with God, the conditions and requirements of this union, amount to a science. It is necessary to allow oneself to be taught certain simple and intangible principles of that science. It would do no good to try to discover it all for oneself.'

At the present time, it is not easy for us to understand the specialist literature about the spiritual life. First of all, we do not have the same cultural background as our predecessors. We have not read the same books, especially Latin works that give the original meanings of the vocabulary, and we have been educated differently. As a result words do not mean the same to everyone. I realised that in a retreat I once did at Paray-le-Monial, where we were given to read some passages from the *Treatise of the Spiritual Life* by St Vincent Ferrer, who died in 1419. The reading had to be abandoned because so many of the participants were shocked by the terminology, even though it was normal in Latin and in medieval writing. The vigorous language of the middle ages could not be understood without explanations. The same applies in regard to many seventeenth century writers: it is so easy to misunderstand them, because we do not know the oratorical style of the time, and we take things literally. Indeed, I know that many of my university friends need a sort of translation before they can accept notions that were quite clear thirty years ago. A young doctor of theology told me recently that he had tried to read a very well-known book on the spiritual life that came out fifty years ago, and he had to give up. There was no connection between his ideas and those of the book. We need to find a language for our own times.

Another problem, it seems to me, is linked with the conditions of life for today's people. We live much longer than our predecessors. Now in the spiritual life there are stages; it is not disconnected from ordinary human life. In the seventeenth century, a person moved almost directly from childhood to adulthood. There was no adolescence in the modern sense of the word. And, at fifty, one was virtually an old person, thinking seriously of death. One had seen people die in one's own house. There was physical suffering that nothing could be done about. Death, suffering, and the inevitable were part of life then, as they still are for those who live in what is called the third world. Today, in our world, people live longer, the stages of life are longer, passages from one stage to another come later. All of which has to be taken into consideration in speaking of the life with God.

Besides, up to recent times, the world was well demarcated. People knew where they came from and where they lived, they knew why they lived and why they died. Their social roles were clear. None of this holds true today. Everyone is obliged, to a greater or lesser extent, to work out his or her own mental framework. There are few if any 'protected areas'. The fluid social ambience has led to lower resistance to certain factors, to greater danger of being harmed, of anxiety, of failures in commitment, of loss of confidence in society, in others, and so in God. This state of mind is intangible but general. There is no point in lamenting it overmuch, but it has to be taken into account in a book of this kind. Aspects of life not dealt with in the old books on spirituality have to be considered, because today's human race is somewhat different, culturally and affectively.

A practical book

Like a traveller's guidebook, I want this book to be practical and easy to use. It is not a neutral book. It is committed to a definite direction in life. It is important to know that. If you read it, you cannot remain indifferent to the itinerary it offers.

I have inserted texts and prayers from other writers in the various chapters. I think that the dialogue between the soul and God will develop more easily with the help of prayer.

In composing the book, I have many people's faces before my mind. May it serve to nurture the love of God and of other people in many hearts, and to open them to the most beautiful thing there is: life with God.

Let us pray the Almighty Lord who changed the desert into a sheet of water, to change our dry soil into a spring; to set about the hardness of our heart and bring it to an end, so that it may change like the rock [in the Bible] into a stream of water. May the Lord pour out on us the dew that drenched the fleece Gideon placed on the ground.[1] We pray that God may enter our garden and drive away the north wind so that the south wind may blow in us, and the seed sown in us be given life by its fertile breath.
St Paulinis of Nola, (+431)

You are holy, Lord God, you alone do marvels. You are strong. You are Great. You are the Most-high. You are the All powerful king, O Holy Father, king of heaven and of earth. You are Three and One, Lord God, all good. You are good, you are all goodness, the supreme good, living and true Lord God. You are charity, you are love, you are wisdom. You are humility. You are patience. You are assurance. You are rest. You are joy and happiness. You are justice and temperance. You are wealth, you are our sufficiency. You are beauty. You are peace. You are protection. You are guardian and defender. You are strength. You are refreshment. You are our hope. You are our faith. You are our great gentleness. You are our eternal life, great and admirable Lord, God almighty, merciful Saviour.
St Francis of Assisi, (1182-1226)

PART ONE

The foundations of life with God

To understand how to live with God, it is necessary to recall first some fundamental points. They are more or less well known by anyone who already has a relationship with him, even if not necessarily expressed in words. But there can sometimes be a drift of ideas that results in false attitudes. So it is best to begin by describing, however briefly, the foundational principles of all spiritual life.

CHAPTER ONE

Why and How God acts

We begin with the action of God in relation to human beings. This can seem a surprising place to start. We might have been expected to begin from the human side since, after all, it is with humans we are concerned.

The important thing to recall is that it is God who is principally concerned with the success of any life lived with him. It is always he who takes the initiative, even if we are not at first fully aware of it. As life with him unfolds, this is something we become progressively more convinced about. It is the framework of this book.

I am well aware that there is a sort of reversal of perspective here. Kierkegaard observed: 'The human person in inclined to relate everything to himself and to relate himself to himself. Think the complete opposite of God.' And St John of the Cross puts it another way: 'If the soul searches for God, God searches much more for it.'

Happiness in God
There is no need to be afraid of what has just been said, as if one was going to be captured by God, to disappear, to lose all liberty and identity because God is leading the soul towards him. That would be a major mistake. Think of a God who passionately desires our happiness: 'In truth, God desires us as if all his happiness depended on it', says Tauler in a powerful phrase.

The first thing to say about all life with God is that real happiness is found there. And incrementally so. It is only when someone lives in intimacy with God that the word 'happiness' receives its full meaning. Everyone who has had experience of that kind of life will agree with me. If you have visited monasteries, you cannot fail to have been struck by the serenity of many of the elderly monks, the calm beauty of so many nuns. Seeing them, one has a real sense of people who have discovered peaceful joy, happiness in God. As the centuries have gone by, artists have taken up this theme. In many frescoes and pictures, the strong and simple sense of happiness emanating from the religious persons depicted is very striking.

There was a time – hopefully, it has passed – when the tendency was to see the life with God as a sequence of sorrows of all kinds. I do not deny that there is real suffering in the life with God, and will return to it later. But it is a suffering that is worth while, and that is far from being incompatible with happiness. The more progress one makes, even if obstacles are encountered, the more positive one's happiness in God becomes.

On the other hand, during the 1960s and 1970s the idea of happiness *without* God was widespread in society, especially among intellectuals. To be happy, it was said, it was necessary to dispense completely with the very idea of God. God was the great hindrance to happiness. This idea still exists, but it has largely given way, by way of reaction, to a certain fading of the thought of happiness. Pessimism, or even collective depression, often prevails today. Bit by bit, the not very attractive contributions of the sceptic Montaigne are coming to the fore: 'If one is building the house of happiness, the biggest room will be the waiting-room'; or, worse still, the remark of Jules Renard: 'No one is happy: our happiness is the silence of unhappiness'. These thoughts are not going to fill us with joy, are they? Unfortunately, there is something of them in the air that humanity is breathing as we begin the third millennium.

In the Bible, God says exactly the opposite. He never ceases to ask human beings to accept happiness. But he also tells us that this happiness is found only in life with God, with him. Happiness consists in the perfect fulfilment of what is within us. But the precise truth is that human beings are made for God, and it is therefore in God, and with God, that perfect joy is to be found.

What this implies is a real break with what stops us going towards God: bad habits, unwholesome pleasures, destructive attachments. Life with God is happiness, but it is necessary to accept a wider and less stuffy idea of happiness than we often have. We often make for ourselves idols of happiness. We pursue false visions and we are amazed when we do not attain them. Happiness is not a sort of virtual reality. It is actual reality, which is what God is. So we are invited to begin by renouncing the idols of happiness. The Jews knew that three thousand years ago:

> *Psalm 16 (15)*
> Protect me, O God, for in you I take refuge.
> I said to Yahweh, 'You are my Lord; from
> You alone comes all I hold good.'
> I am filled with delight by the noble ones,
> The godly ones of the earth.
> Those who follow other gods
> Will find that their sorrows increase.
> I will not pour their libations of blood,
> Nor take their names on my lips.
> O Yahweh, my birthright, my cup;
> You have made my portion secure.
>
> The division of land gave me pleasant places,
> My inheritance is lovely indeed.
> I will bless Yahweh, who counsels me,
> Even at night my heart instructs me.
> I keep Yahweh always before me;
> With him at my right hand,
> Nothing can shake me.
> So my heart is glad, and my spirit rejoices;
> My body also will rest secure;
> You will not abandon me to the grave,
> Nor let your faithful one see decay.
> You will teach me the path of life;

Your presence brings unending joy,
Your right hand grants delight forever.
(tr. Joseph Rhymer, *The Psalms*, St Pauls, Slough, 1994.)

The happiness of God
God desires our happiness because he himself is happy. We associate the idea of God with that of immensity, or eternity, or power. We see God to be a superior being – the Supreme Being, as they said at the time of the French Revolution. We think of him on the basis of what we see to be great on earth, and project it to the extreme degree. It is rare for us to associate God with the idea of happiness, or if we do, we visualise his happiness as a sort of satisfied immobility, completely indifferent to the debates and difficulties of our earthly existence. But is it not our thinking that is wrong?

Basically, what do we know about God? What reason discovers about him. Which, we must admit, is not very much. God is not subject to scientific investigation. We cannot carry out any experiment on him, nor formulate laws about his actions. What is essential and interior to God escapes us.

The faith itself is subject to this limitation of our knowledge. When God says 'I am Who I am' (Exodus 3:14), he affirms his transcendence and places himself beyond all comprehension. The sharpest reasoning puts the matter succinctly: 'God is not eternity, he is not infinity, but he is eternal and infinite. He is not duration nor space, but he exists from all time and he is present everywhere' as, for example, Isaac Newton says. We can speak of the divine perfections, but how can we say more about him?

If we open our eyes, we are not so incapable of saying anything about him. He has spoken to us about himself. The Bible is a long unveiling of confidences about God to us. It has all its meaning and its fulfilment from the coming of his Son Jesus Christ on earth. And this gives us a number of pointers that enable us to go further.

Jesus has revealed to us that God is a single being, but in three persons. First we can speak of the Father in whom everything has its origin. The Father is like an immense heart full of love. God does not possess love in the way we might have intelligence or manual dexterity. God *is* love. He is perfect love, to a point beyond what we can imagine.

Love is linked to life, that is, to gift. It is not closed in on itself, nor does it exist in a closed circuit. It is his very nature. From all eternity, absolutely outside every notion of time, the Father begets the Son to whom he gives all that he is: 'This is my beloved Son to with whom I am well-pleased,' says the Father about Jesus. The Father, then, is all love given, the Son is all love received.

Already, in the relations between the Father and the Son can be seen the notion of movement associated with love. Love is dynamic, living, reciprocal. It brings the beloved ones together: the Father and the Son are absolutely equal and alike, apart from their respective roles of giver and receiver. They are absolutely equal in divinity and still two distinct Persons who are entirely united with each other.

> *Prologue to St John's Gospel*
> In the beginning was the Word
> and the Word was with God
> and the Word was God.
> He was in the beginning with God.
> All things were from him
> and without him nothing was made. (Jn 1:13)

The power of the reciprocal love of Father and Son is such that it is a third Person: the Holy Spirit. It is impossible for us to conceive how a reciprocal love could be a Person. But at least we can wonder at the thought of this power of love in God, at the prodigious potency of this reciprocal outpouring. A hermit has written:

> The Spirit dwells in the Father and the Son: He comes forth from the encounter between them and he is their joy; He is intimacy between the divine Persons, the clasp of their hands, their greeting. The Spirit, at the very heart of God, is

the outpouring of love and happiness, he is their warmth and friendship, the bond that makes them one.²

And a theologian has added: 'The Holy Spirit carries in himself all delight. He arises from the love the Father has for the Son and the Son for the Father. He is the outpouring of their love for each other, or yet the luminosity of their union.'³

Thus, 'each of the Three Persons is for himself only in being for the other two: the Father exists as Father distinct from the Son only in giving himself entirely to the Son; the Son exists as Son distinct from the Father only in being the complete expression of love for the Father.'⁴

In this way the Three Divine Persons live substantially one existence consisting entirely of love in a constant exchange. This exchange is an explosion of happiness, of permanent joy. It is enough for the Three Persons to regard each other: they exist in joy. Trinity is thus an unending song of happiness, a constant exchange of affection. To say God is to say 'happiness', to say 'absolute joy'. To think otherwise of God is to go astray, it is to move away from him and to admit that one does not know him any more.

The happiness that God desires
The Trinity is in no way 'closed' in its happiness. It wishes to communicate it. That is the fundamental reason for the creation of the human race. The human person is created simply to live in love with God, with other people, and with himself or herself. To enter into the luminosity of Trinitarian love is the ultimate end of life. We are on earth only to learn how to live with God, to receive gradually the divine presence and the divine joy, to discover something of God's joy and to share in its stages.

For that, God created the human race in his own image. If we are to live with God, it is clear that there must be something in common between us. 'God said: Let us make man in our image and likeness so that they may have dominion over all the fish of the sea, the birds of the sky, the animals tame and wild and all living creatures on the face of the earth.' (Gen 1:26f)

The creation of man is thus a marvel: it is the crowning, in a sense, of the work of God. But it is necessary to go further and say that God does not create humanity in general: he creates me personally. Just as God is unique, so is every human person, even though we are all of the same race. The wonderful work of God is every human being. So the psalmist could write exultantly:

> For you made my innermost self
> you formed me in my mother's womb.
> I praise you because I am wonderfully made.
> All that you do is wonderful;
> that I know very well. (Psalm 139 (138), 13f)

We shall look more carefully in the next chapter at what constitutes the image of God in the human being, but already we can insist that it is liberty. A human being is only human from being free; otherwise he or she is a machine, guided from without. Unless human beings resemble God in being free, they do not resemble him at all, and so cannot share his life. 'God can only unite himself to gods', writes Simeon the New Theologian. Now, liberty presupposes choice, and human beings have chosen wrongly. Thus, from their very origin, they are cut off from God. They have refused the divine paternity and chosen to create their own laws of life for themselves. That is what can be called 'original sin', or 'the mistaken beginning'.

The sad results of this are all too easily seen. It is enough to consider how people conduct themselves together, and how their capacity for going wrong often controls them. From one point of view, the history of the human race is tragic: 'history' said Pére Lacordaire, is a 'rich treasury of human disgrace'.

And yet, that judgement goes too far. In truth, in different ways God is active at the heart of history. Its underlying movement is the salvation of the human race. Human history is the theatre of the redemption of mankind, of a new action of God that goes even further than creation. It is the history of the adoption of mankind by God, through his Son, Jesus.

In order to save mankind, which was devoting its energies to avoiding its true life, the Father sent his Son Jesus, who became a human being. He became one of us to give humanity back its dignity and its honour, and to open a new way of going to God: 'God became a man so that mankind could become God', as the Fathers of the Church say. Jesus simply repaired the damage we had suffered. He is not a Saviour from outside our race. He is our brother. He took a human body and returned to heaven as a human being.

Through him, humanity in a very real sense enters the heart of the Trinity. There is now a union, a family bond much greater than before, between God and us. This bond is strengthened by a love given to the limit. Christ was not obliged to come on earth so as to save us. He did so because he loved us, because the tendency of love is to bring the loved ones closer together. By becoming one of us, he raised that closeness to the maximum. He was not obliged to die in order to save us. He did so in order to give love to the maximum extent: 'There is no greater love than to give one's life for the beloved', as Jesus says. (Jn 15:13) Once again, at Pentecost, it was through love that he sent the Holy Spirit upon us, so that we could live, here on earth, the love, joy and unity that is the life of the children of God. 'Through the glory and power of Jesus, the most precious, the greatest promises have been given to us, so that you might become participants in the divine nature', says St Peter. (2 Pet 1:3f)

We must place ourselves firmly before this reality: we are of extraordinary value in the eyes of God. How do we know that? Jesus, who is the Son of God, has given his life for us. What could be more significant than the giving of life itself? How could one give greater proof of love? Is it the case that we do not know God, or are afraid of God, or at odds with God? Do we feel unable to approach him? Let us look at Jesus in the crib and on the Cross and remind ourselves that these are realities of the greatest possible significance. God has given his life so that we may have life with him. What desire drives him! What passion – for us!

St Paul's Canticle in honour of Christ
in the Letter to the Ephesians
Blessed be the God and Father
of our Lord Jesus Christ,
who had blessed us in Christ
with every spiritual blessing in the heavenly places.

He chose us in him
before the foundation of the world,
that we should be holy
and blameless before him.

He destined us in love
to be his sons through Jesus Christ,
according to the purpose of his will
to the praise of his glorious grace
which he freely bestowed on us in the beloved.

In him we have redemption through his blood,
the forgiveness of our trespasses,
according to riches of his grace
which he lavished upon us.

He has made known to us
in all wisdom and insight
the mystery of his will
according to his purpose
which he set forth in Christ.

His purpose he set forth in Christ
as a plan for the fullness of time,
to unite all things in him,
things in heaven and things on earth.
(Eph 1:1-13)

WHY AND HOW GOD ACTS

The happiness that God gives

The question now arises of how, in practice, God sets about drawing us towards himself. It is noteworthy how people get the answer to that question wrong, and with what negative consequences.

It is often thought that God acts on us as it were from outside. Sometimes people think that he makes us do this or that, as if we were puppets in his hands. This is quite a widespread opinion. On one occasion I took part with a Protestant pastor in a theological coffee evening where that subject was to be discussed. We were both astonished how many of those who spoke said that they refused to be responsible for their lives. This meant they would not be answerable for anything after their death. But if a person is not responsible for this life, then who lives it, who makes it happen? If it is pure chance, that is incredible. And if it is God, then he is living our life for us, which is an equally terrible thought.

Or else, as is sometimes thought, in a more positive way, God, without determining us absolutely, surrounds us with his protection and his intervention. He creates favourable circumstances and in this way places us in the best conditions for making progress. This is certainly not false. The Bible often says it very clearly. God really does know the needs and risks of our existence, the choices facing us and how much is at stake. He helps us by the permanent ministry of angels. He surrounds us with their protection: 'The Lord has commanded his angels to guard you in all your ways.' (Ps 91 (90):11) The prayer of the saints and of those who love us also plays its part. I am sure that when we go to heaven, we shall be surprised to find how much we have been aided and protected, even in a material way, in the unfolding of our lives. I am even sure that it will be one of our greatest surprises.

But there is more to it than that. God goes much further. This is the key to understanding our life with him: God does not look at us from the outside, as it were. He does not want to have a peripheral contact with us. He wishes to come *into* us. He wishes to be with us in the most intimate and profound unity. He wants really to live in us. And he wishes to do this without violating our liberty, or depriving us of our personality. And indeed he accomplishes this. The result of his mysterious transforming influence is that the more present God is in us, the more we become ourselves, because that is precisely what we are made for. As William of Saint-Thierry says: 'We have been created and we live only for that purpose: to become like him who made us in his image'. And, as Gregory of Nyssa puts it: 'You [human beings] alone of all the universe, are an image of the Being who is superior to all thought, a likeness of incorruptible Beauty, the imprint of the truest Light. By looking towards that Being, you become what he is, because its brightness shines in you, reflected by your purity.'

That is why Christ has come on earth. He did not come so as to save us from the outside, so to speak, but he desires to be a participant in the deepest life of each of us. He wishes to enter our soul. He wants to unite himself to everyone: 'Christ has united himself with every human being', as John Paul II liked to repeat, following Vatican II. That is the whole spiritual life: Jesus wishes to live his life again, as it were, in every life. He wishes us to relive what he has lived, what the seventeenth century French School of Spirituality called his 'states'. Everything that he experienced is given to us, step by step.

This union of Christ with the soul has often been compared to that of husband and wife. It has been explained by commentaries on the Canticle of Canticles, the Bible's magnificent love chant. Origen, St Bernard, and St Thomas Aquinas have written valuable allegorical commentaries on it. What must be said is this: the love of Christ for us, and his longing for union with us, is at least equal to the desire for union between two spouses.

Ultimately, that could make us afraid. Indeed, if we live the life Jesus lived, and unite ourselves intimately with him, we can fear having to suffer with him. But what is most basic in the life of Christ is not primarily his sorrows, but the presence of his Father in his life, and his relationship with the Holy Spirit. It would be good to re-read the whole gospel of St John, which is like a long secret communication from Christ about what is happening within him: the heart of Jesus is entirely occupied with his love for his Father. By accepting Christ into our soul, and re-living his states, we go further and further towards the Father under the influence of the Spirit: 'If anyone loves me,' says Jesus, 'he will keep my word, and my Father will love him and we will come to him and make our dwelling with him.' (Jn 14:23) 'That they all may be one. As you, Father, are in me and I in you, that they may also be one in us.' (Jn 17:21) 'God has predestined us to reproduce the image of his Son so that he may be the eldest among many brothers.' (Rom 8:29)

The life of God, then, is the progressive entry of Jesus into our soul and our increasing resemblance to him. We are 'Christified', 'deified', and adopted by the Father. Christ renews his incarnation in each of us. We become for him 'an extra humanity', as Elizabeth of the Trinity puts it. 'We become children of God if the Word – who became one of us in the incarnation – enters into us and renews for each of us this incarnation; if he comes to share in our individual nature as, in Mary, he came to share in human nature.'[5]

Now, either you have at least the beginning of an experience of that, or else what you have just read will seem to you esoteric, or theoretical, or remote, and you ask yourself the question: 'Is it really necessary for me to continue reading this book?' Think about this before continuing. If you want to go any further read this prayer, which may help you:

> *Reveal yourself in us*
> We do not ask you to renew your birth in human nature,
> but to penetrate us with your invisible divinity
> as you did in a singular way for Mary,
> and as you now do, spiritually, in the church.
> Grant this: may our faith conceive you,
> May our spirit, preserved from corruption, engender you,

> May our soul, always strengthened by the power
> of the Most High, give you refuge.
> *(Prayer of the Mozarabic [Spanish] Liturgy, before 1085)*

THE HAPPINESS THAT COMES TO US WHERE WE ARE
God takes us as we are

One more question remains: that of our unworthiness. Human life is made up of ascents and descents that weigh heavily on us. When we can think clearly about ourselves, we are struck by the distance between the purity of God and the uncleanness of our souls. Even the purest soul is full of sins – except Our Lady.

When one makes a little progress in the spiritual life, this distance causes us pain. Then there comes – or there does not come – a decisive experience, that of the meeting with God's mercy. We must say something about this now.

In a very beautiful retreat which he preached at l'Arche de Saint Domingue, Jean Vanier[6] explained very lucidly that people naturally see the world as hierarchic and vertical. Those with responsibility, those who have the right to judge and assess, are over the others. As a result, in the course of life, we always want to climb upwards:

> The vision of humans, is always that of wanting to climb as high as possible; of winning the race, of gaining power, wealth, dominance, of achieving human glory and renown.[7]

Those who cannot succeed are counted as deficient beings. In extreme cases, they are ignored, marginalised, other people make decisions for them, and if necessary, they are eliminated. They have a diminished personality, if they are recognised as having any rights at all. Now, we often think of God in much the same way. He is the Supreme Being, the God of the philosophers and learned people of whom Pascal spoke; he is the one who dominates, who judges, who classifies. We fear him. Here on earth we can either obey him, not very well, or run away from him, but we always know that he will catch us. But, is that what God is really like? Is this the God Jesus Christ revealed to us?

Against this image of God, voices have been raised like those of Saint Margaret Mary,[8] Saint Faustina Kowalska,[9] Bl Charles de Foucauld, Fr Varillon and Maurice Zundel. The gospel itself teaches us exactly the opposite of our usual vision of God. We learn from it that Jesus has chosen the last place for himself, that he descended as far down as he could, so low that nobody could go further, as Fr de Foucauld used to say. Let us re-read St Paul's extraordinary Hymn to the Philippians:

> *Hymn to the Glory of Christ*
> Though he was in the form of God,
> Jesus did not count equality with God a thing to be grasped.
> He emptied himself,
> taking the form of a servant
> being born in the likeness of men.
>
> And being found in human form,
> he humbled himself and became obedient unto death,
> even death on a cross.
>
> Therefore God has highly exalted him
> and bestowed on him the name which is above every name,
> that at the name of Jesus every knee should bow
> in heaven and on earth and under the earth,
> and every tongue confess that Jesus Christ is Lord,
> to the glory of God the Father. (Phil 2:6-11)

We are shocked when Christ takes on the condition of servant (or of slave: in biblical Greek, it is the same word.) When Jesus washes the feet of his apostles, it is too much for Peter. That is how much the world is turned upside down! It is vital for us to understand this goodness of God, this humility of God who understood people so well that he knew that they cannot be approached from on high. People's pride is so great they will refuse to submit to someone greater than themselves. People's fear is such that they protect themselves with all their power. They are so defensive of their badly employed liberty that they refuse to let anyone approach them. Instead of being the mature individuals they want to be, they are deeply wounded people.

The only way for God to approach us is from below, by being less than we are, more humble, weaker, and dependent on our love. This corresponds to the nature of God in the Trinity. The Father preserves nothing for himself: he is pure movement of giving. He has no superiority over the Son. The Son is pure receptivity. He has nothing of himself, but only receives from the Father. The Spirit does not exist by himself: he is entirely relative to the Father and the Son. The entire life of the Trinity consists in a constant movement of self-emptying and receiving from the other. And that is exactly what love is. If, however, there is distance, reservation, or protection, there is no more purity of giving, of receiving, or of exchange.

On earth, Jesus lived, if one may dare to say so, with his heavenly temperament; he received all and gave all, he protected himself in no way. He wanted to bring about among people the confidence and the defencelessness of the little child. For that purpose, he disarmed himself and became the little child in the crib, he died on the cross without defending himself. In order to come close to human beings, he had to be less than the least, weaker than the weakest, poorer than the poorest.

'Before God we are all poor', Mother Teresa used to say. In the heart of each of us, there are immense zones of poverty. It is precisely there that Christ meets us. He does not meet us only where we are strongest, but where we are least impressive. On the cross, he took all our sins on himself, and knows very well how we stand. In a sense, there are really no rich people, or those who are called such are invited to cease being so: 'Jesus came for the poor, you say. Hé! For sure. But he came for the rich also, so that they might become poor by love, and you cannot be unaware that hundreds of thousands of holy people have obeyed him.'[10]

If we do not accept this poverty of God, we have before us a God as powerful as he is terrifying. And especially, we do not know who God is, because we have not experienced him directly. Jean Vanier explains that, when he asks his L'Arche assistants if they pray, they sometimes tell him 'no'. He asks them why:

And very often the answer is, 'I am afraid to approach God, I am afraid that he will ask me for something that I do not want to do or cannot do.'

As if God were there all the time just to make us do things we cannot do! There is always in us, bound up with our fundamental guilt, this strange idea of a God who punishes and condemns, who wants to take away from us what we like, what we are holding on to, a terrible God demanding sacrifices.

But this is not God!

God is the one who loves us, a merciful God who is never disappointed in us but knows well of what we are made. He knows that there is in us a zone of guilt, a permanent fear of not being loved, a fundamental vulnerability, and that he loves us. He only wants to reveal to us that he loves us, as he said to Peter.[11]

The question of mediations

The revelation of this love is generally made through what are called 'mediations', that is 'means' (Latin: *media*) by which God touches us and builds us up. Indeed, God rarely comes to us directly. Granted, our personal prayer is the basis of our relationship with him. But his graces usually pass through the church that he has founded and that provides us with his holy Word, which she guards and interprets, the seven sacraments, especially baptism, eucharist and reconciliation, and the life of the church generally. I would add that, if someone wishes to make progress, it is necessary to be in dialogue with a good director who knows how to maintain a proper distance.

The aim of this book is not to speak about these 'mediations', which I have dealt with elsewhere,[12] but I would at least recall here their essential importance. Without them, the spiritual life cannot attain its goal.

*

The relationship between God and human beings raises a question of communication. Fundamentally, does God want to have a relationship with humans? Is that what interests him, is that why he created the human race? The Word of God gives a strong and precise answer to this question: the great desire of the heart of God is to have with human beings not simply relations, but a true relation, a relation of the greatest intimacy, going as far as union. God has turned himself towards this communication. He does not put any sense of his superiority into it. What animates him is pure love, as a father loves his children and desires their happiness. That is why Christ came on earth. But, humankind having been created in the image of God, everything depends on our response: 'I have set before you life or death, a blessing or a curse. Choose life then, so that you and your posterity may live, loving Yahweh your God, hearing his voice, attaching yourself to him.' (Deut 30:19f)

As soon as someone chooses life with God, his or her whole being begins to respond down to its very depths. The great adventure begins, people discover themselves as they really are, and the divine heart rejoices in a way beyond our power to imagine.

CHAPTER TWO

How can people respond?

However highly we think of ourselves, we have to admit that we are poorly equipped to deal with this situation. God invites us to become gods by participation, to be adopted by him! Our education has not prepared us ... And yet, the gospel and the tradition of the church leave us in no doubt about the invitation. What can we do about it?

To begin this reflection, we must once more try to switch ourselves away from our self-centredness and consider that God is awaiting us even more than we are seeking God. The following prayer may help:

> *How long you have been waiting for me!*
> O Sovereign Saviour! With what gentleness you have shown your goodness in me! When I did not exist, you gave me existence. I have separated myself from you, and you have not wanted to separate yourself from me ... Lord, how long you have been waiting for me. How often you have protected me! What tender friendship I have found in your welcome! With what goodness you have come mysteriously to meet me! From what evils, from what chains, you have set me free, from what dangers you have enabled me to escape!
> Despite my ingratitude, you have not given up, you have drawn me to yourself, you have given me no rest except in you alone.
> *Blessed Henry Suso (1295-1366)*

THE ART OF BEING A CHILD

Why be a child?
We have seen that God is Father. He cannot be otherwise, and

'fatherhood' is perhaps what defines him best. It is why he creates us and considers us his children. God's parenthood took on totally new dimensions with the birth of Jesus as one of us. To go towards God, the way to follow is that of children. But what that means is not entirely clear.

In reality, one could think that to embark on the demanding adventure of going towards God, one would have to deploy all that is best in oneself, and to the limits of one's energy and capacity. In other words, one should be a responsible woman or man, a fully educated and competent adult.

And it is true that the Bible often tells us to be an up-standing human being and to undertake great things. Courage is especially what is needed. For example, when Joshua was about to begin the conquest of the territory that would become the land of Israel, Moses said to him: 'Be strong and very courageous: you will enter with this people the land which Yahweh swore to their fathers to give them, and it is you who will put them in possession of it. It is Yahweh who goes before you, it is he who will be with you; he will not leave or abandon you. Do not fear, do not be afraid.' (Deut 31:7f) Later, God himself speaks to Joshua and says exactly the same: 'Be strong and very courageous ... Have I not given you this command: Be strong and very courageous! Be without fear or dismay, because Yahweh your God is with you in all your ways. (Jos 1:6, 9) Equally, among women there are examples of great courage, such as Rebecca, Esther, Judith, and, later on, the Virgin Mary. They are praised on many occasions. This courage is often needed to accomplish the works of God, whatever they may be. Likewise, an understanding of life is needed. No one sets out lightly on any dangerous undertaking. Christ himself recalls what the tradition of the church will call the virtue of prudence or of discernment: 'What king who was setting out to wage war on another king would not begin by considering whether he is able, with ten thousand men, to confront one who comes against him with twenty thousand?' (Lk 14:31) The ideal in this matter is King Solomon, full of wisdom in the government of his difficult and complex kingdom.¹

All this shows the role of education and example. Fathers and mothers should bring their children up in this tradition of energy, discernment and faith so that they can accomplish the works of God. And as God told Joshua, his support will not be lacking to them.

All that is certainly valid. Cowards do not inherit the kingdom of God. To achieve anything one must be capable of rational and coherent choice, of steadfastness, of making the necessary sacrifices. Christ confronts us with radical situations. He wants his followers to be men and women who are entirely committed, who are ready to lose everything so as to gain everything. There is no life linked to God without risk and effort. Anyone who wants to embark on that life must mobilise their courage, like Joshua and many others.

Nevertheless, in the search for God, in life with him, there is something even more important than courage, intelligence or ability, and that is the spirit of childhood. There is no contradiction between this and what has been said earlier. As the German theologian Romano Guardini puts it, 'Jesus does not mean anything sentimental, touching, helpless or cute [...] Spiritual childhood, in the sense that Christ intends it, is nothing other than Christian maturity.'² And in fact, the more time passes, the further one goes in engagement with God, the more dominant this spirit of childhood becomes. Why?

Fundamentally, because being human is, structurally, being a son or daughter of God. That is the basic thing about us. The more we advance towards God, the more aware we become of this and the more we want to live it out. We discover ourselves and fulfil ourselves to the extent that the spirit of childhood comes to flourish in us.

Again, it is because human ability and strength is very limited. One begins the spiritual life with all one's energy. One quickly realises that there is no room for compromise in it, and that, in order to progress, there must be sacrifices and losses. But later on, one understands also that the greatest generosity, the best formation and the deepest understanding of life have considerable limitations. One reaches the end of one's capacities. It is a painful experience, but crucial. At that point, there is nothing left except to trust God entirely, to follow the path and to commit the conduct of one's life to him. Then, one discovers the spirit of childhood, and the adult agrees bit by bit to be only a little one. Blessed Columba Marmion expressed that when he said: 'All Christian life and all holiness comes down to that: to be by grace what Jesus is by nature, the child of God ... The highest saint in heaven is the one who here on earth was most perfectly a child of God, who has made ever more fruitful in himself or herself the grace of supernatural adoption in Jesus Christ.'[3] Ultimately, it is all summed up in what the Letter to the Romans says: 'All those whom the Spirit of God animates are children of God. You have not received the spirit of slaves so as to fall into fear; you have received the spirit of adopted children who makes us cry out, Abba, Father! The Spirit himself joins with our spirit to attest that we are children of God. Children, and therefore heirs of God and co-heirs with Christ.' (Rom 8:14-17) Or again, the Letter to the Galatians: 'The proof that you are children, is that God has sent into our hearts the Spirit of his Son who cries: Abba, Father! So you are no longer a slave, but a child; child and so heir of God.' (Gal 4:6f)

This has been the experience of 'the greatest saint of modern times' as Pope Pius XI called her: St Thérèse of Lisieux (+1897). She was proclaimed a Doctor of the Church by Pope John Paul II so that her 'little way of spiritual childhood' might be better recognised and placed before the whole world. What it fundamentally involves is complete confidence in God because he is our Father, and absolute flexibility in his hands. All Thérèse's strength lay in her simple acceptance of her weakness: 'O Jesus, I feel that if you were to do the impossible, and find a soul weaker or more insignificant than mine, you would wish to shower it with even more graces, if it abandoned itself entirely to your infinite mercy.'[4] Thérèse knew that she had nothing, but that God loved weakness. She knew that she was heir and daughter of the King of kings, and that therefore she possessed everything. It was in this way she lived holiness and proposed it to everyone, in its most accessible and at the same time its highest form.

*How Thérèse of the Child Jesus
found the way to become a saint*
You know, Mother, that I have always desired to be a saint, but, alas, I always found, when I compared myself with the saints, there was between them and me the same difference as between a mountain whose summit is lost in the heavens and a grain of hidden sand trodden underfoot by the passers-by. But instead of growing discouraged I said to myself: the Good God could not give me desires that could not be fulfilled, so I can in spite of my littleness aspire to sanctity; I cannot grow bigger, that is impossible, so I must put up with myself as I am with all my faults; but I must seek how to go to heaven by a very straight little path, very short and completely new. We are in a century of inventions, now there is no need to climb up the stairs, because in the houses of rich people there are elevators instead. What I would like to discover is an elevator to raise me up to Jesus, because I am too little to climb the difficult stairway of perfection. Then I searched in the holy books for some trace of an elevator, the object of my desire, and I read these words from the mouth of the eternal Wisdom: 'If anyone is very small, let him come to me'. And then I came, realising that I had found what I was looking for, and wanted to know, O my God! what it is you do for a little one who responds to your call. I continued my search until I found this: 'As a mother caresses her infant, so I will console you, I will carry you on my bosom and dandle you on my knees!' Ah, never had more tender and sweet-sounding words come to delight my soul. The elevator that will raise me up to heaven is your embrace, O Jesus! For that I do not need to grow, on the contrary I must remain little – I become more and more so. 'O my God, you have exceeded

my expectation and I will sing your mercies. You have instructed me from my youth and until now I have announced your marvels, I will continue to declare them until my oldest years.' (Ps 70)

We can become children again
We would very much like to do as Thérèse did. But how can a person become a child again? When Jesus told the Pharisee Nicodemus that be must be 'born again', he retorted, 'How can a person be born again? Can he enter again into his mother's womb?' (Jn 3:1-8) Can someone go backwards – *should* you, even if you could? Fortunately, human nature is well constructed. In the depth of everyone, there remains, without our knowing it, a sleeping child. It remains intact despite the progressive accumulations of life.[5] Contemporary psychologists are aware of this discovery: 'The good news is that we are all born with our sentiments intact. With a little effort and a great deal of courage, we can rediscover this state of innocence.'[6] Dr Vittoz, the great Lausanne psychotherapist, and Dr Tomatis, who has renewed many aspects of our knowledge of hearing, have reached the same conclusion. At our centre there is a three-year old baby, or even a nursling, which is asleep. What we have lived in our early childhood remains engraved on our being, and we can, if we so wish, retrieve this resource.

The characteristic of the baby is to be entirely dependent and to be satisfied with that. In its mother's womb, it is safe. When it is born, if it comes into a normal environment, it is surrounded with care and tenderness, and is given all it needs in due time. It is loved, coaxed, and looked at positively and in a hope-filled way. Later, it has to defend itself and often – but not always – it stiffens up and becomes deformed. What is extraordinary is that it is possible, with God and the Spirit, to retrieve this innocence, this flexibility, this confidence. That is the whole objective of the spiritual itinerary of a human being: to become a child in the Son of God.

Prayer asking for the spirit of childhood
Holy Mary, Mother of God, keep a child's heart in me, pure and transparent like a spring. Obtain for me a simple heart, which does not dwell on sadness, a heart great for giving, tender in compassion. A heart generous and faithful, which forgets no good, and bitterly recalls no ill. Make my heart gentle and humble, giving but seeking no return, glad to lose itself in another heart, before your divine Son. A heart bold and unconquerable, that no ingratitude can close, no indifference make sad, a heart passionate for the glory of Jesus Christ, wounded by his love, with a wound that only heaven will heal.
Fr Léónce de Grandmaison (1868-1927)

ACQUIRING THE REFLEXES OF A CHILD

When someone knows that he or she is a child of God, life changes. Fr Henry Boulad SJ has expressed it well: 'Faith is the certainty of being loved to the point of folly by an almighty Father, creator of heaven and of earth. It is the certainty of being his child. This certitude creates in us the state of abandonment, of relaxation, that transforms our whole being, renews it, regenerates it: one's digestion is better, one sleeps better, one eats better, one looks better, one communicates better, one works better ... Everything changes, because everything in us depends on love. What is needed is that this faith, this certitude, pass over into our body, become flesh and blood and translate itself into our life.'[7]

To enter into the interior life, it is necessary to acquire the reflexes of the child. On the one hand it is necessary to have personal conviction and effort, but on the other it is the Holy Spirit who, responding to our prayer, gives us this gift little by little. What are the most fundamental attitudes of the child, which will gradually become almost like spiritual reflexes within us? We will consider five: confidence, abandonment, desire, attention to the present moment, and purity of heart.

Confidence
A child is confident. To be confident, it is necessary to know that above us there is someone stronger than we are, who wishes us well, who is looking after us, who gives or suggests to us at each moment what we need. This person must be someone who understands us deeply, who knows who we really are, who sees what is best in us. He or she must know our strength and our limitations, and work to give us confidence, to set us free, to challenge us always so as to make us grow. If we have someone like that among our relations, we can rely on him or her.

That is exactly what God our Father is like. To enter into the path of spiritual childhood is to enter at the same time into the way of confidence. Dom Chautard, one of the great spiritual masters at the start of the twentieth century, used to say: 'When you know who God is, when you think about his power and his wisdom, about his love, when you really believe that he is concerned with us at every moment and loves us infinitely, what can you fear?' And with Teresa of Avila we may add: 'God never lets his friends down [...] He never abandons, even if it takes a miracle, those who trust him fully.'

Social life does not always make us confident. There is a delightful little book about French people as seen by English.[8] Chapter 2 is entitled 'Respectful country of mistrust ... and of credulity'. It explains that French people are born and remain distrustful. But in this respect, everyone is of the same nationality! Mistrust is more or less universal.

Now confidence sets the heart free, makes life easy, and gives us a positive outlook on things. To have a positive outlook, to make favourable presumptions, would nearly constitute a mental revolution for most people. But people who have undergone that revolution, and maintained it, know that the polarity of their lives has switched, as it were. The consequences are literally incalculable. To put it briefly, as Thérèse says, 'It is confidence, and nothing but confidence, that leads us to God.'

Abandonment

Confidence leads to abandonment. Abandonment means letting things be. It is no small thing to abandon oneself into anyone's hands, even the Lord's. But after all, when one makes a parachute jump or a bungee jump, or even a plane flight, one has to abandon oneself to 'means of transport' that are purely material. If we really believe in God, if we believe that he is alive, active and has our personal good in mind, why not abandon ourselves into his hands? Abandonment is thus founded on love and on confidence in God, whom we entrust with the conduct of our lives, and especially our inner lives, with a view to going to him.

Abandonment does not mean being indifferent to whatever happens. It is much more dynamic and positive than that. St Vincent de Paul, who practised it a great deal, spoke of it in these terms: 'Perfection consists in uniting our will to God's to such an extent that he and we literally want the same thing to be done and the same thing not to be done.' Thus we voluntarily accept God's will for us. It is in any case quite pleasant to find what God wants for us – it is always for the best. And it becomes clear that the means are to hand and will never be wanting. In this way abandonment makes us go forward with more confidence and more dynamism, greater naturalness and greater drive.

Little by little, it is our whole selves that come to be placed in the hands of God. As Bossuet said, in the striking language of the seventeenth century, 'This act [of abandonment] delivers the whole person into the hands of God, the soul, the body in general and in particular circumstances, all thoughts, all feelings, all desires, all organs and members, all the veins and the blood they contain, all the nerves even the most thread-like, all the bones even to the marrow inside them, all the entrails, everything within and without.'

This could seem somewhat exaggerated. But it makes good sense. Can you say that you know your own psychology completely? You do not. Every human being is a whole world and, as life goes on, we keep discovering in ourselves regions we did not know were there. It is difficult to direct oneself in such half-light. Still less can we say that we know our spiritual world, our soul. Our soul is vaster than our purely human psychology. We do not know where exactly God stands with us, in matters where we obey him, or in matters where we resist him. For the conduct of our soul, the best thing is to hand it over to a good specialist, and the best specialist is God.

It is possible for us to do that because God does not ask us to resign from life or to forego our liberty. He suggests and he inspires from within. He does not force or violate us, because, let us repeat it again, he is a Father. In fact, everything is prepared for us in advance if we choose well. There is great relief in this. As Father Lacordaire said, 'What I know about tomorrow is simply that Providence will be up before the sun.'

For the rest, when we read the gospels, we often find Jesus advising us to let things be, to abandon ourselves, not to worry about what will happen next, to leave ourselves in the hands of the heavenly Father. Jesus himself abandoned himself to the will of the Father in the most terrible moment of his life, when he was most severely tried, in Gethsemane: 'Let your will, not mine, be done.' (Lk 22:42) The Father gave him the strength to go forward to the passion that was to save us all, you and me.

> *Abandoning oneself to Providence*
> Therefore I tell you, do not worry about your life, what you will eat or what you will drink, or about your body, what you will wear. Is not life more than food, and the body more than clothing? Look at the birds of the air; they neither sow nor reap nor gather into barns, and yet your heavenly Father feeds them. Are you not of more value than they? And can any of you by worrying add a single hour to your span of life? And why do you worry about clothing? Consider the lilies of the field, how they grow; they neither toil nor spin, yet I tell you, even Solomon in all his glory was not clothed like one of these. But if God so clothes the grass of the field, which is alive today and tomorrow is thrown into the oven, will he not much more clothe you – you of little faith?

> Therefore do not worry, saying, 'What will we eat?' or 'What will we drink?' or 'What will we wear?' For it is the Gentiles who strive for all these things; and indeed your heavenly Father knows that you need all these things. But strive first for the kingdom of God and his righteousness and all these things will be given to you as well. So do not worry about tomorrow, for tomorrow will bring worries of its own. Today's trouble is enough for today. (Mt 6:25-34)

Desire

Abandoning ourselves into the hands of God does not make us inactive. We change over, as it were, into a different mode of action. If we believe that everything depends on us, we deploy everything we have and drive ourselves very hard. But if we know that God is doing the main work, we will continue to do our part, while above all asking our heavenly Father to give us what we need. Asking, expecting and praying become priorities. They come ahead of action, but they do not block it.

There is no asking without the expectation of being heard. That is why desire is so important in the spiritual life. A person who lives with God is a person of desire. He or she stretches out for what God is going to give, which means firstly God himself: 'Like the deer that yearns for living streams, so my soul is thirsting for you, my God', as the Psalm says. (Ps 42-3 [41/2]:2) Desire arouses confidence. Nothing contributes more to spiritual growth than desire for God and his blessings. And the more we have, the more we desire God: 'To progress unceasingly towards God and never to give up, that is really to enjoy the Well-Beloved; the fulfilled desire of every moment calls forth the desire for what remains beyond,' says Gregory of Nyssa.

If we meditate attentively on the Our Father, the perfect prayer that Jesus has taught us, we see that Christ seeks to increase without limit our desire for God. Certainly, the Father knows what we need, and wishes to give it to us day by day. But he also wants us to desire it and to ask for it. Otherwise, we would become spoilt children, who think that everything is our due. The Father gives us everything, but he gives it to children happy to receive it, who understand its cost, because they have desired and sometimes waited. Desire prepares appreciation for the value of things, and makes us grateful to the Lord. We are children who are satisfied, but who, because we have desired, are also grateful children.[9]

Attention to the present moment
Everyone knows that a little child lives in the present moment, does not think of tomorrow, because his father and mother think about that for him. In fact we have only one day before us. Who knows where we shall be tomorrow? Why trouble about what we will be doing then?

Unfortunately, one of the things that paralyses, or at least greatly interferes with the action of God in us, is flight. We flee from God because we flee from reality. The grace of God is ready for us, but when it arrives we are not there. We have gone away. We have left the present moment, and fled into the past or the future, in memory or imagination ('the fool of the house' as Malebranche calls it). The real is sometimes so hard and agonising that we run from it. We do not want to accept it. We try to drive it away from us. Virtuality does not help us to be incarnate, to keep our feet on the ground. Flight from reality is also the deep reason for drug-addiction, alcoholism and numerous other deviations. We are often, at least to some extent, aliens in the midst of our own lives. And then suddenly we are no longer alive.

Going towards God supposes an effort to abandon the virtual and to enter the real. This effort is possible if we have confidence in the value of the real, if we know that God is waiting for us there and will satisfy us there – and nowhere else. The real is the instant in which I live, here, now. The past is dead, and will not come again. The future is not yet and may never be in the way I expect. Only the present is real and God is nowhere else except in the present. Unless we understand that we will not live. We will pass our lives in a sort of dream and we will die having by-passed the beauty of real life.

Jean Vanier tells a story on this point:
There is a young boy in the school who is always saying, 'Ah! When I have left school and am at work, I shall be happy.' He left school, and began working, and always said, 'Ah! When I get married, there will be happiness then.' He got married and after some months he realised that life was boring and he said, 'Ah! When we have children it will be good.' The children came, and it was wonderful, but they sometimes cried until two in the morning, and the young man sighed, 'If only they were grown-up.' And then the children grew up, no longer cried until two in the morning, but did a thousand and one foolish things and real problems started. Then he dreamt of the time when he would be alone with his wife: 'Then it will be grand.'
And when at last he was old, he thought nostalgically of past times, and said, 'It was fine back then.'[10]

Take heart! Let us not fear the effort of being converted to the real. Joy is there, happiness waits for us, because God is there, and also those whom he will give us to love. Let us come out of our incubator, and enter real life.

Purity of heart

In the Sermon on the Mount, which is more or less the beginning of Jesus' preaching in St Matthew, Christ gives pride of place to what we call the Beatitudes. (Mt 5:1-12) One of them is this: 'Blessed are the pure of heart, for they shall see God.' Seeing God is thus linked with having a pure heart. This is very important for our purpose.

Purity is the opposite of impurity. Impurity can relate to the body, but notice that Jesus here goes deeper and speaks of the heart, which in the Bible is the centre of the human person. It is the location of intimate thought and fundamental decisions. Impurity is linked with having: I put others and God himself to my own use. I turn them towards myself; I do not recognise them; I do not respect them. I make objects or even machines of them. My heart is full of myself, it is not free; there is no place in it for the grace of God, it is not pure; I cannot see God. I think myself strong, but I am blind. I have put myself in the centre of the world and I think myself rich, but I am the poorest of the poor, only I do not know it. I have by-passed real life, without knowing that it even existed.

In this matter too, we are called to a process of conversion that is to last for more or less the whole of life. But already, at the start of the whole spiritual journey, we can commit ourselves to it in good faith. When Jesus met Nathanael for the first time he said to him, 'Here is a true Israelite, in whom there is no guile.' (Jn 1:47) He did not say that he was competent, that he was capable, that he would be a great man. He said he was a man of good faith, who sought God's will more than he sought himself. The education of Nathanael, like that of the other apostles, took three years. There will be moments of progress and moments of doubt, and Nathanael, who will take the name of Bartholomew, did no better than the others at the time of the Jesus' passion. But at least, in the midst of his difficulties, he will remain a man of good faith, unlike Judas, whose heart was not pure. That is why he will receive the Holy Spirit and set out to preach the gospel.

God makes saints out of poor people. But he wants people of good faith, of pure heart. A prayer that asks for purity of heart, insisting on receiving it little by little, is one that God will never refuse.

> *What purity of heart consists in*
> Purity of heart consists in having nothing in the heart, which could be opposed however slightly to God and to the operation of his grace.
> All the creatures in the world, everything in the order of nature and of grace, the whole conduct of Providence, tend to take away from our souls what is contrary to God. For we will never arrive at God, until we have corrected, cut back, and destroyed, whether in this life or the other, whatever is contrary to God ...
> When the heart is well purified, God fills the soul and all its powers, the memory, the understanding, the will, with his

> holy presence and his love. Thus purity of heart leads to divine union, and ordinarily one does not arrive at it by other ways.
>
> *Fr Louis Lallement (1588-1635)*

THE ZONES OF BEING

Now that the reader has – I hope – been convinced of the basic principles of the human response to God's call to life with him, it is necessary to consider the structure of the human being especially as it is related to God. A short outline of theological anthropology will be very helpful for understanding how the grace of God manifests itself, and where the movement in the spiritual itinerary takes place. For this purpose we will use what is known as the schema of the 'zones of being'.[11]

Description of the zones of being
It has always been known that in the human being there is a body and something more. This 'something more' consists of the capacities that go beyond the body: intelligence and the capacity to choose or the will. Deeper still, it is known that there is in the human person the capacity to enter into relationship with God. That capacity is called the soul. St Thomas Aquinas, following Aristotle, but completing him and making him more precise, has given the most widely accepted treatment of the subject. Finally, it is also known that the human person is capable of remembering a great deal of what has happened to it. Bergson even said that we are capable of remembering everything, and that the problem was not to explain remembering but forgetting. This capacity is called the memory. There are therefore several ways to describe the human being, which do not contradict each other.

Let us note from the outset that the human being is both one and diverse. It lives in the present, but it has memory. It acts at any given moment more in the body, or more in the intelligence, or in the will, or in the soul, but all the rest is still there and active. The human being is always a unit, a person, formed of complementary elements like the members of a body.

Let us also note that this is a good thing in itself. The human being has been willed by God to be so and created by him under this form. It is how it is constituted. Christ took our humanity when he took on all that makes a person human. So we must set aside, at the point we have reached, every thought that affirms that the human being is deficient. It is, on the contrary, very well made, although it is damaged. It has all that is needed to progress, but it often chooses to go backwards. The whole aim of the spiritual life is to put things back in the right way. It can be seen that everything is in order and works well, once some necessary corrections have been made. It is rather like physiotherapy.

Several zones can be distinguished in the human person which, it must be noted from the start, are isolated from each other, but in constant communication. The 'zones' do not however have the same degree of 'depth'. One could even say that there is a certain order of importance among the different zones. That is certainly the case as far as the spiritual life is concerned.

The first zone, the most 'external', so to speak, is the body. It has its own life, its needs and its reflexes. It also has its memory. The second zone is the sensibility, that is to say the way in which one feels what concerns the body. The third zone, more 'developed', more internal, is the intelligence. At the centre is the 'I' or the 'deep self'. All these zones are affected, each in its own way, by a person's relation with God.

The body

The widespread idea that the body is exterior to the person and an obstacle to the spiritual life must be dismissed from the start. *'Le corps, c'est moi'* – 'I am my body.' I am not a soul imprisoned in a body, which seeks to get out as soon as possible. I am a soul and a body together: a soul does not exist without a body on this earth. No body, no soul.

The body gives me my place in the universe. By its matter, it puts me in relation to matter. It inserts me into time, and even no doubt into long and mysterious biological time. Its interior rhythm is very important for the spiritual life: the rhythm of days and nights, the rhythm of season, the rhythm of ages. Through the senses it puts me into contact with the world and with other people. The good use of the senses establishes one's proper distance from the world and from others. For example, a beautiful sound well modulated finds a strong and positive correspondence in me. The body is thus a space for dialogue and a capacity for action. It is always awake, even (relatively speaking) at night. It is always directed to the exterior, and conveys information unceasingly. The body is an essential instrument of dialogue: 'All that I am resides in my body. Touching my body is touching me in all my being. Running away from someone's body is distancing yourself from them on the emotional level. In our society a handshake expresses openness and social proximity to the other. When someone refuses to shake another's hand, it tells him that there is an obstacle in their relation.'[12] So it is not surprising that life with God takes the body into account.

Certain forms of modern psychology, picking up a biblical point, have shown that there is a certain symbolic function for the body. In other words, each part of the body is linked with the sensibility, as it quite clear, but also with the intelligence and the soul. If I place my hands on my heart, it is not a neutral gesture. By doing so, I show that I have something deep in myself, that is capable of being reached and touched, in one way or another. The way people breathe, the rhythm of their breathing, can also bring them to something very important for themselves in terms of their vitality and the foundations of their intimate life.

The body has its own needs. This raises a problem. Because the body is tainted by sin, its needs can at times become tyrannical and uncontrolled. They make powerful demands. That is what St Paul means when he writes in agitation, 'Who shall deliver me from this body of death?' (Rom 7:24) The need for food, the sexual need, and so on, can lead to a loss of control. That is why the body needs to be dominated, right throughout life. Christian tradition and common sense, as well as many historical philosophies, explain that it is not necessary to grant the body everything it demands. It is necessary to educate it. Experience shows that this can be gradually achieved

Note finally that the body has its memory. It remembers everything that has touched and affected it: sicknesses, acts of tenderness, acts of love, attacks. Contemporary psychology insists on this point, which, to go by my experience, is extremely important for the spiritual life.

The sensibility
The sensibility is a capacity to interpret what is felt by the body. For example, if I hear a noise, I do not remain at the purely acoustic level. I decode it. I decide whether it is positive or negative, good for me or a threat. It will give me pleasure, or make me afraid, or do nothing at all because I have no clear consciousness of it. The voice of a friend not heard for a long time will arouse in me a positive emotion, while an aggressive shout on the metro will arouse the opposite feeling. Each time my body provides information, my sensibility decodes it by the aid of its own memory. Sensory memory is very strong and active in the human being. Whether I want to or not, whether I show it or not, I live to a great extent at the level of the sensibility.

The sensibility therefore occupies a very important place in human life. Everyone knows how different it is in men and women, among different temperaments, at different stages of life, and according to each one's personal history. The sensibility in itself is positive and willed by God. It goes far beyond the body. It colours in a very personal way what reaches us from outside ourselves. It can be an extraordinary way of transmitting expressions of love. It should not therefore be judged negatively. There is nothing more terrible than a person who has tried to suffocate his or her sensibility, not least because it is impossible: the sensibility can only be buried.

The sensibility is both something beautiful, and a source of danger. It is so personal that it easily becomes subjective and, like the body, reaches the point of being tyrannical. Unless care is taken, the sensibility can dominate our vision of the world. We can come to function on the level of 'I like' or 'I don't like', and short-circuit the stage of reflection. It can give us a very fine view of the world, but on the other hand it can close us entirely in on ourselves, making us egotistical. Like the body, it needs to be converted so as to operate harmoniously, which, once more, takes time.

Intelligence
When we come to intelligence, we enter a more complex world. It requires a great deal of time and effort to 'bring up' an intelligence, [to form a mind]. Intelligence does not simply mean what is recognised by way of academic grades. As the La Garanderie method shows, every child is intelligent in his or her own way. There are many forms of intelligence and academic grades only refer to some of them. It is necessary to say this, because in present-day society, the opposite is often thought.

Intelligence is not the capacity to pass examinations, but to know the real, to take up a proper distance from it, to reflect on it. The real means not only the material world or social organisation, but the meaning of life and the way to live. Intelligence supposes a certain distance, [abstraction], it introduces elements of comparison, that is to say, discernment and a culture. It draws on the body and the sensibility, but it goes much further, thanks to its capacity to generalise, and develops concepts and lines of reasoning, as well as generating explanations and proofs. The memory of intelligence, like that of the body and the sensibility, naturally plays an essential role in the process of thought.

There is no spiritual life without intelligence. We must become children again, but not become animals. There is an intelligence of faith, of the life with God, which is given to simple people, in simple forms, but which supposes nonetheless attention and the marshalling of thought. This is why Fr Clérissac could write: 'Christianity is the religion of the intelligence.'

The work of the intelligence is very satisfying when it is well done. It is more objective than the sensibility. Intelligence is the capacity to attain truth, and is linked intrinsically with the real. The sense of being intelligent brings a person to a higher level and enables him to breathe more freely. But intelligence still belongs to a wounded being, and is capable of being deformed, of making mistakes. It can easily be conquered by pride and immediately becomes unreasonable. The myth of Doctor Faustus expresses what can happen. We can become stupid by thinking how intelligent we are. We then truncate the real, and live in a world that is disconnected and dangerous. The history of contemporary humanity affords many examples of such dangers.

So intelligence too needs to be purified. This is a delicate matter, because it is often thought not to be necessary. The submission of the intelligence to the real and to God demands time, sacrifice and a readiness to grow in humility.

The 'deep self'

At the centre of the human person is an extremely important zone, which can be called the 'I', ['ego'] or the 'deep self'. It is the place where I recognise myself fully, the place where I find my freedom. It is where the most fundamental decisions are taken, and where God resides. It is sometimes called 'the soul', or 'the centre of the soul'.

We have already spoken of the soul. In a general way, the principle of life of a living being is called a soul. It is the 'form' of a living body, that is to say it makes it what it is, an organised body endowed with life, not a simple conglomeration of elements. In the same way, the human soul is the 'form' that makes the human body to be what it is: the body of a human being. But, as we said at the outset, a human has capacities of its own that surpass those of matter, however organised. It has therefore a spiritual principle of animation. This spiritual soul is created immediately by God, and is immortal: it survives the body. But, at the same time, whatever the body experiences impacts on the soul in one way or another. The intelligence, for all its dependence on the data of sense and conditioning by the brain, is fundamentally a spiritual capacity, irreducible to its organic conditions. Intelligence cannot be reduced to the 'processing of data' such as a computer can do, nor to the sensation and the instinct of animals. A human being *thinks*, that is to say, it is capable of taking an interest in things as they are in themselves. It asks itself questions about its own being and the meaning of existence. Capable of reflection and abstraction, it also has a sense of good and evil, of justice and injustice. It can be bound by a promise. These are all things of which animals are not capable, and which give evidence of the reality within it of a spiritual soul, transcending the purely organic faculties.

The central capacity of the soul is the capacity to make free choices. Exterior forces do not control the soul, even if they influence it. It remains always an interior place, which nothing can destroy, where I can make my most fundamental choices and accept my responsibilities. This capacity is called the will, which is a 'driving' power, a dynamism, people's ability to orient themselves towards their end, their goal, like a compass pointing towards the north, while leaving them with the power to choose.

In this centre of the soul is also found the place of life with God. Here we touch on a matter about which much has been written, but which remains very mysterious. Let us state some points that seem to be incontrovertible.

First, if the soul is made to receive God, its capacity is immense. The greatness of the soul is without doubt infinitely greater than we could know in the world of matter. The spiritual life therefore unfolds in vast horizons, which we only explore in part. Saint Teresa of Avila, at the beginning of her *Interior Castle*, or the *Book of Mansions*, expresses magnificently the beauty and the greatness of the human soul: 'Today [...] I find before my mind what will be, right from the start, the basic point of this book: consider our soul as a castle built entirely of a single diamond or a very clear crystal, where there are many rooms.' Then, she insists that the soul is a sort of paradise, because God wishes to dwell there, and adds: 'I do not see anything that can be compared to the great beauty of the soul, and to its vast capacity.'

Nonetheless we are not completely ignorant of what happens in the soul. God's action in us is perceived by a 'sensibility' of the soul. The Fathers of the Church spoke of the spiritual senses. They said that just as the body has five senses, so the soul possesses spiritual senses that permit it to hear, to smell, to touch, to see and to taste God. As the spiritual life develops, the spiritual senses come into play. They unfold under the influence of grace. It is an immense surprise to see them develop one after another. Gradually a 'spiritual consciousness' comes about. Just as I can be conscious of my acts and thoughts, so I can become conscious of the action of the grace of God in me, even if this awareness remains extremely limited. The soul thus discovers itself little by little under the action of the Holy Spirit.

The soul then discovers something else: namely, the faculties that are linked with it, of which we spoke above. The will and the intelligence are the faculties linked with the soul, and God acts in them. Finally, there exists as it were a memory of the soul, which recalls all that God has done in it. God is at work in the faculties, occupies them, purifies them, modifies them.

To the extent that the action of the Holy Spirit unfolds in the soul, it becomes more and more the centre of the life of the person. The French use of the phrase *'une âme'* ['a soul'] to mean 'someone' shows well the esteem accorded to the soul as the living centre of the person: the same usage is sometimes found in English. But the soul never leaves the body, nor does it destroy the sensibility or the intelligence. She is master of them, animates them with a new life, which is the life of the Holy Spirit.

We said that the soul is a world, and we said also that it has a centre. The spiritual life, is progressively directed from this centre, which is a place of unity, a place of extreme peace, like a lake of calm water, and also a place of deep simplicity. To go down to the centre of one's being in order to meet God and to live with God there is the whole programme of the spiritual life. That is the destination of every spiritual journey.

*

When one has had some experience of human existence, one sees that it is admirably designed and made for entering into a relationship with God, living with him, becoming his child, and walking with him in the way of love and peace. The human person is indeed a being capable of God, in the sense of having the capacity to receive him.

The problem is that people are not aware of that, and when they are, they prefer to stay on the margins of life with God. They consider what they would have to give up in order to go towards God. They do not agree to enter into this programme of renouncing their limitations so as to aim at farther horizons. If only people knew what they are losing by remaining at the level of the earth! The truth is that life with God, real life, lies completely open before us. It is the stages of this life that we are going to examine.

PART TWO

The Stages of the Spiritual Life

The spiritual life is life as lived under the guidance of the Holy Spirit. In it, the Spirit's influence is more important than human activity. It is also unpredictable. There is no point in attempting to forecast what will occur along the way. The unexpected is one of the decisive factors in life with God. So extreme flexibility is of the essence of the spiritual life.

Nonetheless, from very early times, it has been known that there are a number of stages in life with God, and that there are certain common traits in the experience of different people. There have therefore been attempts at describing these stages. St John Climacus for example gives no fewer than thirty-three steps in his *Mystical Ladder* leading to the contemplation of God. But that is perhaps too complicated. A synthesis was gradually reached that concentrated on three stages: that of beginners, that of the proficient, that is, those making progress, and that of people who are living in full union with God. Within each of these stages, certain degrees have been identified. In my opinion, it is St Teresa of Avila who has done this most successfully, in her *Interior Castle*. She has not covered everything – there are certain types of experience she has not described – but still her general teaching is valid, so long as care is taken in choosing the words that will communicate what she says in today's language. For example, we shall not use the old words 'purgative' and 'illuminative' for the first two stages, because of the negative connotations they can have. So I have preferred St Augustine's terminology ('beginners', etc,), as above, to that of the writer known as Pseudo-Dionysius ('purgative', etc.)

CHAPTER THREE

The Beginnings of the Spiritual Life

As we begin these chapters, I would with to repeat that they should not be read too rigidly. God's way of acting is immensely flexible: 'The distinction between the three ways (the three stages) should not be overemphasised. For one thing, all authors are in agreement that there is no high point of the spiritual life from which one could not fall. For another, God can without doubt, in certain more or less exceptional cases, lead a soul without any apparent intermediate stages from sinfulness to great sanctity.' But especially, there is interaction between the various stages. 'The distinction that matters is rather that of predominant aspects of the spiritual life at one or other of its stages than of strictly successive elements.'[1]

I would also advise refraining from judging either oneself or anyone else. Life with God remains extremely mysterious, and human nature also can be very surprising, for better or worse. Our judgements are limited. A certain humility and purity of heart are essential if we are to be open to what God has prepared for us.

THE FIRST DWELLING-PLACES: AT THE DOORWAY TO THE SPIRITUAL LIFE

In her book *The Interior Castle* or *The Dwelling-places*, St Teresa of Avila compares the soul to a magnificent castle, where the King of kings lives. We are invited to go through it step by step. It is clear that as we reach the more interior parts of the palace, the closer we come to the master of the house. I am going to follow her exposition in a general way, because, as already mentioned, it is the one that I personally find best.

THE BEGINNINGS OF THE SPIRITUAL LIFE   59

The danger of the life of sin

The First Dwelling-places concern those who have not yet really begun the spiritual life, because they have not made a conscious choice of ascending towards God. Evidently this is a very varied condition, concerning a great many people. There are those in the first place who are far from any spiritual life because they are trapped in the opposition to God that is linked with sin.

At the start of her *Interior Castle*, St Teresa of Avila speaks of souls who find themselves as it were on the path that skirts round the outside of the castle. They do not pray to God in any personal way, and they are very sinful. They are, as she puts it, 'absorbed in worldly affairs, engulfed in worldly pleasure and puffed up with worldly honours and ambitions'.[2] She adds that they are 'paralysed', or 'crippled', living as it were surrounded by vermin.

That description probably fits a great many of us. We often live for ourselves alone. Consciously or otherwise, we choose either not to believe in God, or to live as if there was no God, or to give God a secondary place in our lives. 'I am the centre of my world.' Not many would put it so bluntly, perhaps, but it is how we live. I see others as dependent on me, and I make them revolve around me. God is far away, and his action on me is, at most, vaguely protective. My only aim in life is my personal interest. And, as a result, I have no taste for God. He is not part of my inner dynamic. The 'divine good', anything to do with God, produces nothing in me except a permanent unhappiness.[3]

I once had a conversation with one of the major booksellers in France about the pattern of sales in his enormous shop. He told me which types of books sold most. At the end, I asked him, 'Could you sum up in a word what people at present are looking for when they buy books?' He answered at once, 'Yes, absolutely! They are looking for themselves. The world of most people is like a circle with themselves at the middle. That is what the publication and advertising of books take for granted. Society is so individualist that everyone puts himself or herself in the centre of the world and relates everything to themselves.' The ideas of self-gift, of generosity, of self-denial, of sacrifice, of effort, of progress towards God and others, of forgiveness, are all either wiped out or relativised. If you do not believe me, ask yourself whether the official teaching given to children is not oriented in this way.

Self-seeking can take many different forms. But in fact, we are not that interesting to ourselves. Since I am made for God, my interior capacity is huge, and my own ego cannot satisfy me for long. I soon grow tired of myself. At that stage, I try to find fulfilment in social recognition, in money, in sex, in escaping into drugs or alcohol, and so on. Gradually, I set up a deformed version of myself, a sort of manageable deviancy. I can pass on from small sins to more habitual sins and ultimately to serious and permanent sinful conditions. 'Let us beware of things while they are still of minor importance,' says Dorotheus of Gaza,[4] 'lest they become more serious. Otherwise we run the risk of falling bit by bit into complete spiritual insensibility.' The problem with the condition of grave sin is that in it I no longer receive any enlightenment. This attitude of profound deviancy is called in the Catholic tradition 'mortal sin'. As the book of Esdras puts it: 'Here we are before you, Lord, in our guilt, though no one can face you because of this.' (Esd 9:15)

Grave sin is all the more serious because everyone is a wounded person in one way or another and, if I do not go towards God and towards others, not only do I fail to receive healing for my wounds, but in the end I begin to be driven by those very wounds. I add to them, not alone in relation to myself, but to others. I become dangerous. That is often seen in the matter of violence or of sexual deviations: I do what has been done to me. Ultimately, locked into an infernal circle, I can become brutalised in wickedness and unhappiness, an individual or even a collective 'structure of sin'.

A person in this condition does not have enough enlightenment to see the truth, or enough discernment to distinguish good from bad. The spirit of confusion is dominant, and evil spirits have free play. They hold in their grip those in this desperate situation.

THE BEGINNINGS OF THE SPIRITUAL LIFE

The lukewarm life

Fortunately, not everyone is in this state. But there are many others who, though not completely cut off from God, have not made the choice of advancing towards God either. They are living in a sort of compromise, in an attitude that is neither cold nor warm. They are divided between the values of what St John calls 'the world' and the call of God. The values of the world are all the things society sets as goals: wealth, success, enjoyment, and so on, which do not go in the direction of total self-gift to God.

Normally baptism is the start of the spiritual life. In baptism a child is given and receives faith. After that, this grace should be developed by means of a Christian education, prayer and the sacraments. And then, once the stage of first childhood is over, there are personal choices to be made. Sooner or later, the time comes for a fundamental choice: What will I build my life on? No one can escape this choice: as Hans Urs Von Balthasar puts it: 'Jesus Christ requires everyone to choose, acceptance or refusal, faith or denial of faith, concern for God's glory or concern for one's own glory.'

Thus, on the basis of what one had received as a child, one can make a decision to consider God as the essential and first thing in life, and to go towards God. Many souls set out on this path. For them the Christian life is in direct continuity with their baptism and their initial education. If they have a sense of making effort, of self-giving, of generosity, and are not too taken up with themselves, then they are attentive to the calling of God, they go forward gently, and then one day they tip over into the feeling for God. But sadly not everyone makes that choice, either because they find mediocrity preferable or because they do not really understand what Christianity is about.

So, there are Christians whose spiritual life remains mediocre. They pray a little or hardly at all. 'I have not murdered anyone, I have not stolen anything', is what they say. They are satisfied to remain at ground-level. They do not understand those who want more, they criticise them. There are lives where God is not absent, but which are heavy, narrow and without the happiness that the relationship with God provides. They believe in God, but drag their feet because they do not realise that God is already present, at this moment, unexpectedly, as someone alive in my life. They hang back. They keep telling themselves, 'No point in doing anything, because it gets you nowhere.' This luke-warmness is a terrible thing, because it wounds the Heart of God and prevents any spiritual development.

The question remains the same for a person who was not baptised as a child or given a Christian upbringing. A choice of God needs to be made. In their case it is harder, and it is less clear what the spiritual life might consist in. A person is less distanced from the 'world' and does not have any other values to refer to. There is no light for them to see by. At the present time there are many conversions. Those who meet God in this way often say: 'We were never told that God really exists.' This is why evangelisation is important. It may not necessarily convince people, but it can offer light to people who might be glad to accept it.

The zones of being and the First Dwelling-places
In this first part of the spiritual life, there is always a certain amount of imbalance between the different zones of the personality. Often, the corporal zone is disproportionately large. It can dominate everything, everything can depend on it, particularly in what concerns sexuality. It is as well to acknowledge that. But at other periods of the spiritual life or for other people, the sensibility may be what is predominant. Everything can be related to it. One of the problems of the sensibility is that it can easily become a virtual world: it can isolate people from reality and lead to illusion. For example, a marriage predicated solely on the sensibility will face difficulty.

It can also happen that the intellectual zone predominates. This is more subtle, but happens more often than might be thought. It means that the whole world is placed in relation to what I happen to know about it. It is measured according to my sphere of competence, which I myself over-value and even absolutise.

Behind all this, deep needs lie hidden, desires for recognition or for love, and resentment at injuries suffered. The difficulty becomes greater because, when one zone of the person's being is given undue prominence, it does not communicate well with the other zones or give them the attention they need. They then become weakened. In particular, the 'deeper self' is no longer fully engaged. I revolve on my own axis but can never become myself, because it is only by contact with God that I can really find myself and fulfil myself. On the other hand, when the 'deeper self' is actualised, all the other zones are gradually affected and given their proper place.

Setting out on the road towards God
Is God absent? No. Even in this first part of the spiritual life he is much more active than might be thought. First of all, he protects people and saves them from a worse fate. Many of the conversion stories people tell show that. Then, he arouses certain souls in a hidden way to pray for sinners and to make sacrifices for them. Undoubtedly this happens a great deal. And finally he sends people rays of light, and draws benefit from whatever good and whatever opportunities arise in their lives.

The day comes when one realises what one's situation is, and wants to get out of it. It could be a sudden illumination: God comes crashing in. The history of the church, even its recent history, is full of sudden conversions. St Paul is always the best example. Sometimes, the conversion is slower, more gradual, as in the case of St Augustine. But the most important thing is coming to understand that illumination is possible, that there is a way forward. Then we know that God exists and is waiting for us. Then the journey can start, at a quicker or slower pace.

To make progress, what matters most is desire. Teresa of Avila cried out, 'I want to see God.' Perhaps at this stage of the spiritual life, not many would express themselves like that, but at least there is the desire to progress, to go towards the light, to make a move. There will be a beginning of conversation with God, that is, of prayer. It may not be clear that he is listening. He is asked to prove himself. In this way the possibility of communication opens up. And it is noticed that life is out of shape – that it contains some major blockages. Then comes the desire to free them up, and discovery of how to do so. A start is made. Then, if someone keeps to the road, everything may be hoped for.

> *A Prayer for Encouragement*
> 'Even in the abyss, I passionately loved you.'
> O Truth! Light of my heart! I allowed myself to sink into my darkness and my sight was obscured. But in the depth of this abyss, yes, in the very depth, I loved you passionately. Even when I was lost, I remembered you. I heard your voice behind me, calling me to come back, but I misunderstood you because of my unappeased passions. And now, here I am, drowned in sweat and out of breath, returning to your living waters. Let no one stop me! I will drink them and then I will live.
> St Augustine (354-430)

THE SECOND DWELLING-PLACES: THE BEGINNING OF THE ROAD

Some general points

The Second Dwelling-places are already some way into the castle, even if still in the outer rooms. The people in those rooms want to progress towards God, and take the proper means to do so. They begin living in God's presence, and are in regular contact with him in prayer and the sacraments. It is as if there were a channel or a line for them between heaven and earth, along which grace is starting to circulate in an almost regular way. But the relationship with God is not steady. It is wavering. There is a conflict between what is calling me forward and what is dragging me back. The desire for God is there, but not yet readiness for the necessary sacrifices. Pleasure, self-fulfilment, and the values of the world in general often still drown out the voice of God. It is a case of being pulled one way and another. All the time God is present, his importance is realised, there is a desire not to abandon him, but not a great deal of strength.

THE BEGINNINGS OF THE SPIRITUAL LIFE

This is how St Teresa of Avila describes those involved in the Second Dwelling-places: 'They are people who have already begun to practise and who realise the importance of not remaining in the First Dwelling-places, but who are often not yet resolute enough to leave those Dwelling-places, and will not avoid occasions of sin, which is a very perilous condition. But it is a very great mercy that they should contrive to escape from the snakes and other poisonous creatures, if only for short periods, and should realise that it is good to flee from them. In some ways, these souls have a much harder time than those in the First Dwelling-places; but they are in less peril, for they seem now to understand their position, and there is great hope that they will get further into the castle still.'[6]

They are in pain because they are torn in two directions. They have not yet completely made up their minds. But still they know what they have left behind and do not want to go back to it. They are divided against themselves, because being far from God they do not ask themselves questions. They are somehow open to evil. God's entry into their life has not given them rest, but rather disturbance. The devil, knowing human weakness, takes advantage of this. He raises powerful interior temptations, reminds people of their former pleasures and suggests going back to them. He makes use of friends and relations who do not understand how they have developed and do not approve of their spiritual advancement.

Here is another disconcerting element: it is part of life to seek pleasure. That is an interior structure, an aspect of human psychology. There is an unconscious tendency towards the permanent satisfaction of the ego. A person is now beginning to know God, and hears Christians and people already converted saying that this life with God is marvellous and full of joy. But precisely at this second stage there is no joy. One is naturally aiming for a new kind of pleasure, but the impression is of toppling into emptiness. This seems unbearable. Then comes discouragement, feeling either that all the talk about a life of happiness with God is false, or that 'such a life is not for me'. To quote

St Teresa again: 'Here we are, meeting with hindrances and suffering from imperfections by the thousand, with our virtues so young that they have not yet learned how to walk – in fact, they have only just been born: God grant that they have even been born at all! – and yet we are not ashamed at wanting consolations in prayer and complaining about periods of aridity.'[7] It is quite shocking to see people who have begun on the way of spiritual life, who have begun to pray, who receive visible favours from God and even charisms,[8] but who compare life with God with that of the world and finally choose the latter. They drop into a kind of obscurity that leaves them with a taste of sadness and failure, until they find themselves 'de-converted' and face to face with great emptiness.[9]

Happily, God is there. The Lord 'so much appreciates our love for him and our seeking his company that he never fails, from day to day, to call us and invite us to come to him.'[10] In other words, grace is not lacking; we are not abandoned to our self-doubt and our limitations. Likewise God provides the friends and the support that is needed. If we want it to, our relational world can progressively change. The Lord gives us assistance in that regard. He cannot allow us to lose out in the confrontation with ourselves, with the world and with the devil. He tips the balance with his power. True, in this situation we often do not know where he is or what he is doing. We as yet lack the sensitivity to recognise him. But he is very present all the same, and sends the strength and encouragement needed. In particular, he counteracts and limits the action of the devil: 'God is faithful: he does not permit you to be tempted beyond your strength; but with temptation he gives you a way out of it and the strength to endure it.' (1 Cor 10:13) Our will is always free. If it continues to choose God, we shall go forward little by little. We will not spend our whole life in the Second Dwelling-places if we have the courage to go further.

Building an interior world
It may be wondered why God has us pass through these Second

Dwelling-places and not move forward faster. The reason is the necessity of building our interior dwelling-place on rock. Life with God is very strong and powerful, it transforms the person in depth. Unless we build on a solid interior world, life with God cannot last, and we will fall. It happens that people receive great spiritual graces and charisms, even publicly visible ones, but regress suddenly and completely. I have seen that happen.

So it is necessary to be modest, humble and patient. In general, it takes a good number of years to lay and lay again the foundations of life with God. How is it done?

Quite simply, exactly as in sport: by way of practice. God brings progressively to our attention the points to work on. We take one, and apply ourselves to it. Then we go on to another, and so on. Our psychology gradually takes on a good shape. Our faults diminish and start to disappear. As time goes by, things get easier, the stronger and freer we become, and the struggle becomes less, at least in certain areas. The sporting metaphor was already used by St Paul, and it is in fact very relevant.

> Do you not know that in a race the runners all compete, but only one receives the prize? Run in such a way that you may win it. Athletes exercise self-control in all things; they do it to receive a perishable wreath, but we an imperishable one. So I do not run aimlessly, nor do I box as though beating the air; but I punish my body and enslave it, so that after proclaiming to others I myself should not be disqualified.
> (1 Cor 9:24-27)

The first point to work on is contact with God. This is established by the conversation with him that we call prayer. It is necessary to pray faithfully and regularly each day, to pray with the church by participating in the liturgy and receiving the sacraments,[11] to pray with fellow-believers as the occasion arises, whether in a prayer group or in an ecclesial community. Sometimes it will seem that nothing is happening, that God is as it were dumb. Perseverance is needed then. In such moments of aridity, when nothing is felt, the will is obliged to make choices:

'I want to continue praying, I want to choose you again.' By means of these choices the will strengthens itself powerfully. It becomes more and more strong and sure of itself: it matures.

The second point to work on is our inner self. In other words, it is necessary to replace bad habits with good habits. In the classical tradition, the latter are called 'virtues', and they are aspects of our being. It is traditional to distinguish them into the virtues necessary for our life as a child of God, the 'theological virtues' of faith, hope and charity, and the 'cardinal virtues', those needed for the human conduct of our life, namely, prudence, justice, fortitude and temperance.[12]

The theological virtues are not in the first instance the fruit of our own efforts: they are gifts of God. But they develop by way of our acceptance of them and our determination to grow. For instance, charity, the virtue of love, is not just a good feeling that we may or may not have. It depends on repeated choice: that of loving God, in the first place, and then that of loving others, and when necessary forgiving them, even if they do not love us. If we take the decision to love, our inner world is enlarged, and we even feel that the capacity of our heart is increased. Faith too is made stronger by being practised, that is to say, by praying and by overcoming doubts. Likewise with hope. That is a virtue that can increase to an extraordinary extent when we place our hope in the power of God and not in the capacity of human beings.

Prudence is not cowardice or hesitancy, but the virtue of good self-government: what should I do, what am I capable of undertaking? It is linked with intelligence and experience of life, but God perfects it by his grace, if we pray for its growth. We do not always have inspirations from heaven, but God acts through our intelligence, from within. Justice is not linked necessarily to legal proceedings: it is the art of giving everyone what is due to them. It dislodges us from being centred on ourselves. I do not simply take whatever I want, but first consider the needs of others (and my own) in an objective way. Fortitude is an absolutely indispensable virtue, because on it depend fidelity and perseverance in what we undertake. Fidelity, humble fidelity, is the very basis of all spiritual life. As for temperance, it is the virtue of balance. It avoids all excess and all loss of control, which need to be carefully guarded against. It also safeguards us against the temptation of thinking one is a saint too quickly. A person can have moments of fervour, which is all to the good, but one should not jump to the conclusion that one has arrived. There is still some way to go.

The great virtues are accompanied by a number of smaller ones, which place us in contact with other people, with God and with ourselves. Lists of them exist, but everyone can make his or her own list. It will include the fundamental attitudes of human and Christian life: for example, respect, politeness, attentiveness, generosity, joyfulness, peace, mercy, openness with others, service, piety towards God, appreciation, bravery, purity, and so on. Everyone will have his or her own particular attraction among the virtues, but in fact when an effort is made at any of them, there is progress in all of them, step by step. It is a whole education, and therefore takes time.

The spiritual combat
It must be admitted that the Second Dwelling-places are not only a place for laying foundations, but also a battlefield. This is something to be conscious of and not afraid of. It is God's battle rather than that of human beings: God is more concerned than we are with the outcome. It is necessary to labour and not seek for rest, to fight and not to heed the wounds. The mercy of God is always there to heal us. Relative failures should not disturb us. If we do not give up or grow discouraged, we will always go forward, even if that means sometimes falling.

In the spiritual combat, a person learns gradually to control his or her inner world. One asks oneself the following questions: 'What is it that I accept into myself, especially images, ideas, and suggestions? What are the ideas I like to consider, that I always come back to, and the images that continually crop up? Are they good for me?' This line of thought leads gradually to self-mastery. The various zones of being start to take their proper places, and develop harmoniously in relation to each other. Memory is purified. I am more in control of myself. I know where I am going and how to get there and by what means. This is a part of life where it is often a question of action, and I have a sense of achieving a great deal. It is necessary not to become a voluntarist, that is, someone for whom action is everything, otherwise one would never get beyond the Second Dwelling-places, but it seems true that human activity is of the greatest importance.

The Interior Combat
The person engaged in the spiritual combat should always have four qualities: humility, a high degree of attentiveness, aggression, and prayer. Humility because the combat sets us against demons, who hate humility, and keeps us within range of the heart of the Lord, who hates the proud. Attention, so as to exclude from the heart any evil thought, however good it might appear to be. Aggression, so as to drive the evil one from the field with ferocity. And prayer after the combat so as to cry from the depths of one's heart to Christ, with inexpressible groaning. Thus the combatant will see his enemy and all his imaginings disappear at the holy and adorable Name of Jesus like dust in the wind or smoke.

The innocent child lets itself be seduced by the trickster, and in its simplicity follows him. Likewise our soul, simple and good as its good Master created it, finds the suggestions of the demon attractive, is seduced and runs after the evil one just as if it were good. It mingles its own thoughts with the imagination proposed by the demon. Whether it is the image of a beautiful woman, or something completely against Christ's commandments, the child seeks a way of putting into action what it has seen. It identifies with its thought, and actively performs to its own condemnation what it has mentally seen.

This is how the evil one proceeds: it is with these arrows that he poisons all his victims. So, it is more prudent, when the spirit does not have long experience of warfare, not to let thoughts enter one's heart. In particular, at the very begin-

> ning, when our soul feels attracted to the suggestions of demons, takes pleasure in them and follows them eagerly, it is crucial, as soon as one notices these thoughts, to drive them from the field at the very moment they reach us and we identify them.
> *Hesychius the Sinaite (VIII-X century)*

Do not remain alone. Ask God to bring you into contact with a group of motivated Christians. The first advantage of this is getting better advice, and discerning more easily, with the help of others, the areas to concentrate on, the steps to be taken, and wrong turnings to avoid. Being in such a group protects people from illusions regarding their internal state, and from the scruples that can torment some hearts. The group can keep its members better informed about the good and bad aspects of society. Thanks to others, someone can begin a new way of life, or even acquire a new culture. The example of others can encourage a person to progress. Seeing the incredible advances they have made invites one to equal their achievement.

Vocation and the Second Dwelling-places
In my view, it is possible to receive a vocation at this stage of the spiritual life. The word should be taken in the wide sense: it could be the vocation of marriage, of consecrated life, of the priesthood, or entry into a community, or taking up one or other form of activity willed by God. The vocation can be entirely authentic and its fulfilment may begin. There is no need to be perfect in order to listen to the voice of God and set out on the road.

The communities and church groups to which we can belong serve, at this stage, to form, structure and sustain us in the spiritual combat. Each person has his or her own graces, into which they are invited. A church group is engaged in a project given to it by God: so it offers an ideal to be attained and arouses people to generosity and commitment. It proposes means suitable for this goal. As a result, no one needs be isolated or obliged to discover everything for himself or herself. There is something like a rule of life that involves a long-term plan and makes fidelity easier. Often there is personal accompaniment or at least principles of evaluation that save us from subjectivism. This encourages people to go beyond their passing moods, impatience, fear or repugnance, and to move forward steadily. The different groups in the church, communities and movements, are thus providential aids to progress in the spiritual life.[13]

THE THIRD DWELLING-PLACES: A STATE OF RELATIVE EQUILIBRIUM

What are the Third Dwelling-places?
Gradually, one succeeds in overcoming the first obstacles to life with God and reaches a more stable condition. The choice of God has now been made. The Lord has been given first place in one's life. 'In enabling souls to overcome their initial difficulties, the Lord has granted them no small favour, but a very great one'.[14] The soul has reached self-mastery, the practice of regular prayer, has set up its Christian life in all its modalities, often belongs to a group in the church, is not marginal in society, is active in its own life, and has the awareness of being responsible. We are now dealing with an adult, who has put order on his or her life. St Teresa of Avila gives a pleasing description of such people: 'I believe that through his goodness, there are many such souls in the world: they are most desirous not to offend His Majesty; they avoid committing even venial sins; they love doing penance; they spend hours in recollection; they practise works of charity towards their neighbours; and they are very careful in their speech and dress and in the government of their household if they have one.'[15]

This life is based on regular contact with God in prayer. The prayer is of an organised and active kind: there is reading, meditation, intercession and conversation with God. Sometimes a set method is followed, sometimes the person develops their own. There is awareness of the importance of the Word of God and of the sacraments. Once it has become an established practice, prayer is easier. The person at this level is very committed to prayer, and likes it. There is concentration and recollection in it. 'The soul... gathers all its powers and retires within itself with its God'.[16] This is not the result of God taking control of one's life. It is the result of a good habit of mind and a self-mastery that is able to concentrate its attention on something it loves. There are moments of very pleasing fervour. At times, if one is touched, for example when meditating on the passion of Jesus, there may be tears. There are sometimes feelings of deep absorption, when the prayer descends more deeply into the self (this is called prayer of recollection).

Likewise, there is an awareness of sin. The conscience becomes more sensitive. There is the desire not to live in recurring sin, and to find ways of avoiding it. The devil is less in control, and his frontal attacks can be identified.

There is also a readiness to learn and to perform works of service. One's thought is more coherent, with something of an implicit theology. Life is judged by reference to the Christian faith. Positions are taken up that do not necessarily harmonise with what is 'culturally correct' in the milieu.

Again, there is a sense of the importance of the church and a desire to serve God by means of it. Ways of getting involved in what needs to be done are sought out. There is generosity, and what one does is often appreciated.

As St Teresa of Avila said, there are probably many people in this situation. I am convinced that a good many practising Christians, including young people and even children, are in this category. So also many priests, many consecrated persons, many seminarians, many members of communities and ecclesial movements. 'This is certainly a desirable state,' says St Teresa of Avila, 'and there seems no reason why [those in it] should be denied entrance to the very last of the Dwelling-places; nor will the Lord deny them this if they desire it, for their disposition is such that he will grant them any favour.'[17]

The charisms
A 'charism' is a gift of God given to someone for the service and

the building up of the church. It is independent of the virtue of the one who receives it: it is a genuine gift. But, if the charism is lived with a good will, it also builds up the one to whom it is given. It impacts, in a way, in all the virtues. A charism may not last for the whole of a lifetime: that depends on God's will.

Certain charisms are 'mystical' in nature, and we shall speak of them later. Others are more simple, and are sometimes given as early as the Second or the Third Dwelling-places. For example, the charisms of service and of welcoming: a person feels drawn by God in this direction, and finds all the abilities needed to assist others or to make them feel welcome, which up to that were not part of their nature. Others receive the charism of counsel in one or other area, of joy, of calming people's minds, of making contacts with people, of decoration, of financial administration, and so on. When one considers any group of Christians, one sees how numerous the charisms are, even if they are not always spectacular. The task of building up the church should largely consist in utilising the charisms discerned and encouraged by those in authority. That brings satisfaction to both those who have the charisms and those in authority, and thus spreads happiness all around.

The limits of reasonableness

Fr Marie-Eugene of the Child Jesus has rightly called the Third Dwelling-place 'the triumph of reasonable activity'. That is at once the strength and the weakness of this state.

It is a strength because it gives one a good sense of himself or herself. One knows one's capacities and limitations. There was a struggle to get to this point, and it has now been reached. The bodily zone is in its proper place, and likewise the affective zone, or so one believes. The intelligence knows why one is alive and what one should be doing. The whole being is mobilised to a large extent, and it responds to what is expected of it in the domain of social and personal religious life.

The weakness is that one is sometimes too reasonable. There is often here an unconscious pride based on personal certitude and the sense of knowing what matters most. There is the feeling of having 'arrived' and being able to judge the world and others by one's own measure, swiftly. It is often a case of being a distinguished Catholic. People like this are certainly adult, as they must be, but they have not yet become children. They do not understand those who have done so, and judge them severely. Pride is not dead. There is impatience with trials, especially with difficulties in prayer. If prayer becomes more difficult, if it is hard to concentrate, there is the temptation to reduce or to give up the time set aside for it. When difficulties arise, as they always do, one becomes disconcerted.[18] An exterior orderliness of life can deceive others as to the quality of the virtues and how deeply they are rooted, but they have not yet reached the depths of the soul. Attachment to God is real, but the attachment to self is even more real.

As well as that, there are whole areas of oneself that one does not know about or is even running away from. People are afraid of their wretchedness. Sometimes it becomes clear with age or contact with certain circumstances. People have within them areas of malignancy and weakness that are masked.

The parable of the rich young man (Mk 10:17-22) is expressive enough of the state of these souls. From one point of view they are rich, they have 'great wealth'. The life they are living is admirable, something to rejoice in, but it is not epoch-making. It remains largely human. They admire the saints, but they feel that sanctity is not for them. The call of the great beyond holds no appeal. Yet, sometimes, they feel in the depth of their souls a breath of God inviting them to other horizons. Something in their life is trying to lead them into a new place. For that they will have to go beyond reason to the heart and to a little folly, involving a form of impoverishment for the sake of a new kind of wealth.

*

All spiritual writers have encouraged souls to progress. The apostle Peter said: 'Grow in the grace and knowledge of our Lord and Saviour Jesus Christ' (2 Pet 3:18), and Paul wrote to the

Thessalonians: 'Finally, brothers and sisters, we ask and urge you in the Lord Jesus that, as you learned from us how you ought to live and to please God (as, in fact, you are doing) you should do so more and more.' (1 Thess 4:1f) 'There is no limit to this kind of progress. No limit can stop the progress of someone ascending towards God, because, from God's side, there is no boundary, and from the other, the growth of desire for him cannot be ended by any satiety', says St Gregory of Nyssa.

One could say to oneself that in going like this towards God, one was risking all. It would mean losing some of the familiar land-marks of social life, abandoning the logic of the 'world', and placing oneself in the hands of an unseen being whose demands could be limitless. Once again, it must be said that it is something we can do only because God is good and because God is Father. We can do it because we are animated by love. He has already proved that to us, has he not? So we can take risks for God. Our recompense will be at the level of our risk.

> *What have we risked for Christ?*
> What have we risked for Christ? What have we given him on the basis of his promise? The apostle said that he and his brothers would be the most wretched of men if the dead were not going to rise again. Can we, in some way, apply that to ourselves?
> *Cardinal John Henry Newman (1801-1890)*

CHAPTER FOUR

Progressing in the Spiritual Life

A new state of mind
In the stages of spiritual growth that we are now about to consider, we are dealing with the spiritual life proper, and entering into the intimate dwelling-places of the castle, where we will really come to know – albeit progressively – the master of the house. He has brought us into a very close relationship with himself. The Bible expresses something of this by using the language of lovers, such as we find it in the Song of Songs ('the Most Beautiful Song'). Only the language of love can convey complete intimacy, although it is necessary of course to understand it in a metaphorical way. In the part of the spiritual life we are now going to study, it is important to be on our guard against false mysticism, which is quite widespread. It consists in unduly favouring the zone of sensibility in our make-up, without recognising that the spiritual relationship with God is at the level of 'the deep self'. God himself will provide any other purification that is needed, as he knows best, with everything being transfused by a deeper and deeper love.

> *From the Song of Songs*
> The voice of my beloved!
> Look he comes,
> leaping upon the mountains,
> bounding over the hills.
> My beloved like a gazelle
> or a young stag.
> Look, there he stands
> Behind our wall,
> Gazing in at the windows,
> Looking through the lattice.

> My beloved speaks and says to me:
> 'Arise, my love, my fair one, and come away,
> for the winter is past, the rain is over and gone.
> The flowers appear on the earth;
> the time of singing has come,
> and the voice of the turtledove is heard in our land.
> The fig tree puts forth its figs,
> and the vines are in blossom;
> Arise, my love, my fair one, and come away.
> O my dove, in the clefts of the rock,
> in the covert of the cliff,
> let me see your face, let me hear your voice,
> for your voice is sweet, and your face is lovely.
> (Song of Songs 2:8-14)

We are, at this stage of the spiritual life, more and more convinced of the love and the action of God, because we have some experience of it. We have gone from the shadow into the light, and we have a much better-founded faith. More darkness of course awaits us, but it is completely different from the darkness of sin, doubt and the absence of faith. The difficulties do not extinguish joy, which becomes more and more dominant.

What happens may be expressed like this: God takes over the conduct of operations. For that purpose, he installs himself, with our agreement, in our 'deep self', the depth of our soul. The Holy Spirit, little by little, comes to be our guest in an ever deepening way. From the centre, God penetrates progressively into the different zones of our being. He goes, that is to say, from the centre to the periphery. He 'divinises' and, more precisely, 'Christifies' our whole selves to an ever greater extent.

It is amazing to watch and still more to experience this movement. Far from closing us in on ourselves, as oriental meditation techniques often do,[1] this action of the Spirit opens us more and more towards God and towards others.[2] Far from making us resistant to feelings, or indifferent, this penetration by the Spirit of God leads unto greater sensitivity. But it is not disturbing, because we realise more and more that God is Father. We no longer fear him, but allow him to act upon us with great openness and contentment.

THE FOURTH DWELLING-PLACES: A NEW BEGINNING

The out-pouring of the Spirit

At a certain point, something happens to our spiritual lives. The relationship with God changes completely and, as it were, a new world begins. It is almost as if heaven touched the earth.

After years of prayer and effort, or suddenly and without warning; at a stroke or step by step; as the result of community prayer or quite unexpectedly, God reveals his presence in a way that is new and evident. He is there, before me, in me, at home with me. I do not see him with my bodily eyes, but his presence is such that I cannot doubt it. He is, as Blessed Elizabeth of the Trinity puts it, in 'the heaven of my soul'. This presence has an unbelievable power. It is at once completely surprising, disconcerting and reassuring. It is fulfilling beyond description, in a kind of explosion of joy, that lifts one above oneself. There is the sense of having come into port, or finally having found true life. The image may be used of finally meeting a beloved person with whom one has communicated for a long time only by messages. Then they come into our garden, tap on the window-pane, and are there before us.

This is not the result of a process of thought or any exercise of intelligence. It is far beyond that. The powers of the spirit that are at work are quite different, and are at the centre of the soul, in the deepest part of the 'deep self'. The eyes of the soul awaken. The spiritual conscience appears and becomes fully active. I am able to see another world, and I know it with certainty.

Often, this new life has a face, involves a meeting: I have 'met' Jesus. I move from a rather distant and obscure relationship with God to an 'immediate' and close relationship with Jesus, the Son of God become a human being, my friend and my brother. I know who it is, and he has really become 'someone' for me. He has not actually appeared to me, but that does not matter: the effect seems to me to be the same. I have passed from the stage of a faith that depends on a certain reasoning to one that 'sees' (comparatively), experiences, and tastes. Jesus has showed himself with the power and the beauty of his being. He calls me, he asks me to follow him, and I have no trouble doing so. He is so close and so attractive! The word 'incarnation' takes on its full meaning for me. One could speak of an 'unveiling': the curtain separating heaven from earth has opened for me. I experience what those on the journey to Emmaus did when they recognised Jesus actually with them. The eucharist acquires a completely new dimension, whether the Mass and communion, or adoration of the Blessed Sacrament, and I now understand effortlessly what it really means. Sometimes, this presence of Jesus does not leave us throughout the day and night. The body sleeps, but the eyes of the soul are always awake. When one awakes, Jesus is there!

This experience of the meeting with Jesus is frequent at the present time. Sometimes, less frequently, it is a meeting with the Father that opens the door to the really spiritual life. Sometimes again, it is the Person of the Holy Spirit who reveals himself. And sometimes it is the Divinity in itself that signifies its presence, without the divine Persons identifying or revealing themselves as such.

When it happens, my life is totally transformed. I can never be the same again. I am completely renewed within myself. I enjoy a peace that goes to the depth of my being: it is as if a lake of peace had established itself in my innermost soul, which can never be troubled if I really want it so. The fear of hell or of the risks involved in contact with God disappears. So does the fear of death or of anything that could happen in this life. Naturally, the nerves and the imagination are not completely convinced. But the depth of the soul knows that God is master and that everything works for good for those who love God.

Another result of this encounter with God is a new generosity. One makes a new gift of oneself. I am ready for anything. Huge undertakings do not frighten me. I can make myself available for any sacrifice. Nothing seems difficult to me, because Jesus is with me and is constantly helping me.

A third immediate effect of this meeting with God is joy. This is not human joy, which is sometimes the result of some effort, but the joy of Jesus himself, which penetrates the heart and the entire being. The heart expands in a new way, beyond the sensibility and the intelligence: 'It is not', as St Teresa of Avila puts it, 'a matter of thinking much, but of loving much.'[3] What one feels is that one is discovering new horizons of love that leave far behind anything experienced before.

Other people often notice that something has happened. No one however can really understand it unless they have experienced it themselves. So one's companions can be at a loss. They can think you have fallen in love. If you try to explain it, the reaction will often be sceptical, or negative, or envious. I am no better than anyone else, and yet something has happened to me from which they feel excluded. People will think me a bit odd, especially at first, if the transformation is so great that I change my vocabulary or my attitude. Unless someone helps me, I may even think myself a little strange. But I cannot deny that Jesus is there, in my life, present and acting: and this without any merit on my part, or anything that compels him to do this for me. We are in the presence of a completely gratuitous gift of God. We can only concede that it has happened and submit to his will. In the league-table of virtue, I am not very far up. Nevertheless, it is to me that this has happened.

In a religious community, great respect and prudence will be needed when one of its members has this experience. If people are afraid of it, if people want to keep him in the ordinary path because they fear he may be a victim of false mysticism, if he is told to keep on praying just as before, a great deal of harm may be done to his soul: he may be slowed down, or even broken in spirit. Superiors who are too rigid or, on the other hand, too enthusiastic, can be dangerous in cases like this, and there is no substitute for experienced spiritual guides.

The experience may come to someone who has been walking with God for a long time. Sometimes years go by without God revealing himself. As St Teresa of Avila said, '[It does not matter] when the Lord is pleased to grant these favours, for no other reason than because His Majesty so wills. He knows why he does it and it is not up to us to interfere. As well as acting, then, as do those who have dwelt in the Dwelling-places already described, have humility and again humility! It is by humility that the Lord allows himself to be conquered so that he will do all we ask of him, and the first way in which you will see if you have humility is that, if you have it, you will not think you merit these favours and consolations of the Lord or are likely to get them for as long as you live.'[4]

We should state however that if someone receives this 'gift of the Spirit' without having previously lived a Christian life, he or she should start living one forthwith. It is like restoring a masterpiece that has been painted over. Nobody is dispensed from the practice of virtue or from effort, even if they have this experience at the beginning of their spiritual journey. They need to work seriously and without discouragement and, perhaps, for a long time in order to validate what they have received. For others, those who have taken great trouble to lay the foundations of the Christian life, this meeting with God is not the obligatory outcome of the process, but a marvellous revelation of what the period of preparation meant.

Movement into passivity

One of the most spectacular manifestations of this new closeness to God is the movement from activity to passivity: God takes charge of operations and I follow. But it is important to understand what exactly this means.

God takes command in a way that is more or less direct. It is a new world, his world, and he is master. All the texts of the Bible that deal with the sovereignty and omnipotence of God, with Providence and with the priority of his action, will speak to us. We know well that we have received all that we have, that nothing human could produce it, that we depend on him for everything. Gradually, the action of God will penetrate everything and move forward. God will increasingly ask us to consent, to abandon ourselves to him, to let ourselves be dealt with. For those around us, if they are not tactful regarding people's inner lives, that could be a worry.

For all that, activity does not vanish. Often it is more appropriate and more effective because – as we shall see later – the Holy Spirit is directing it. But it can be said that one has passed from the well-known schema 'See, judge, act'[5] to the schema, 'Pray, discern, obey.' Passivity is neither resignation nor illusion. It means being given the strength and enlightenment that will make activity more powerful. This is the time when God uses people to achieve great things, because they will be doing his work in the way he wants it done. No longer is it a human work, part of a human project, but God's work being done by human beings who are capable of hearing him and giving him their consent. What happens is the movement from doing work *for* God to doing the work *of* God. Listening to God, turning the ear of the heart towards him, becomes one's basic attitude in action.

That brings great happiness, *but it is not easy*. In our world, it is not what we have been led to expect, and it is not the natural tendency of human beings. This is the reason why God will train us himself in ways we shall consider further on.

The transformation of the life of prayer
The life of prayer could not escape the general transformation of the person's life at this stage, inasmuch as prayer is the point of privileged contact with God. Prayer thus becomes easier, is as it were a gift, and brings great happiness, because in it one effortlessly 'feels' God as present and revealed. St Teresa of Avila devotes great attention to the difference between the satisfaction found in the active meditation of the previous Dwelling-places and the consolations given freely by God in the Fourth.

In prayer, passivity becomes essential. Formerly, prayer was organised, structured. One knew what one wanted to do; at the end of prayer, one could go back over what one thought. Now it is not the same. The prayer does not come from us, but is given directly by God. This is so surprising that sometimes one would hardly want to call it prayer: 'Nothing happens when I am at prayer.' If one is asked, 'But was God present?', the answer is: 'Yes, all the time, more and more, in a way much better and different from before.' One feels so happy during these periods of prayer, which in any case seem to go on all day! It is as if one is always in the presence of God, in contact with him, in conversation with him, but without gabbling, and always understanding what he is saying. Thanks to prayer we move effortlessly into a gentle peace, a sort of quietude. Teresa of Avila even calls it 'the prayer of quietude'.

To compare this new form of contact with God with that of the preceding Dwelling-places, she uses the celebrated image of the two basins of water: These two large basins can be filled with water in different ways: the water in one comes from a long distance, by means of numerous conduits and through human skill; but the other has been constructed at the very source of the water and fills without making any noise. If the flow of water is abundant, as in the case we are speaking of, a great stream still runs from it after it has been filled; no skill is necessary here, and no conduits have to be made, for the water is flowing all the time. The difference between this and the carrying of the water by means of conduits is, I think, as follows. The latter corresponds to the spiritual sweetness that, as I say, is produced by meditation. It reaches us by way of the thoughts; we meditate upon created things and fatigue the understanding; and when at last, by means of our own efforts, it comes, the satisfaction which it brings to the soul fills the basin, but in doing so makes a noise. In the other fountain the water comes direct from its source, which is God and, when it is His Majesty's will and he is pleased to grant us some supernatural favour, its coming is accompanied by the greatest peace and quietness and sweetness within ourselves.'[6]

Strangely, this prayer is sometimes perceived as being beyond thought. One is aware that it is in the depth of the soul that it is happening, and not just in the intelligence or the imagination. As a result, at times, there is no thought. There can be distractions, 'one can be thinking of something else'. It can be surprising. One is present, at prayer or adoration, aware of the presence of God, in no way denying his presence, but never, as formerly, being able to pull oneself together, to concentrate. And yet still one knows that one is at prayer. It is like being in two different worlds, the human and the divine. When one is not accustomed to this state of things, questions may arise and one may be worried about oneself. But there is no real division within the person, nor is there anything unusual happening. One is simply exploring a new zone of one's being, 'the deep self'. Thus, 'it is not good for us to be disturbed by our thoughts or worry about them in the slightest; for if we do not worry and if the devil is responsible for them they will cease.'[7] It can all be part of the spiritual combat. The devil disturbs us to make us slacken in our progress towards God. If he finds us quite at ease, he will give up, and our resistance to him will contribute to our progress. So let us make up our minds not to be disturbed by any distractions.

I said above that this prayer is, as it were, independent of thought, above it. That is why one seems at times to come back to very simple kinds of prayer that can even seem like a regression. For example, people may cease to meditate systematically, because they cannot, and go back to saying the rosary. This prayer to Mary can seem 'primitive', without any thought of what one is saying, a succession of 'Hail Marys' on which the mind gets no grip. But at the same time one is well aware that the heart is awake, and that prayer is going on gently and continuously. It is the same with the recitation of the prayer of the Russian pilgrim: 'Lord Jesus, Son of the living God, have mercy on me a sinner.' It is all a gift of God. If one forces oneself, the outcome is not good. It is better to let oneself be 'without violence or noise', to direct the will and the inner gaze towards God as much as one can, and not to struggle with thought.

Prayer beyond Thought
Eternal one, I am silent; in your holy presence, I do not dare to breathe; and my soul, in silence, admires the greatness of

your glorious name; what shall I say, deep in this endless ocean? While your clarity floods us to infinity, can we as much as open our weak eyes?

... I come before you trembling, O inaccessible light; and without seeing the incomprehensible one in his depths, in astonished flight I flit around.

Leave off, what can you expect from your incertitude, your vain thoughts, vain efforts, useless studies? It is enough that he has said: I am who I am. He is everything, he is nothing that I think, with these deep words, I adore what he is, without thinking about it, or imagining that I am on his track ...

... Come down, divine Spirit, pure and heavenly flame, powerful driving force of the hearts I secretly weep for; And you who bring the Spirit forth in everlasting rest, grant to my powerless soul your presence; make of it, as you are able to, a faithful loving soul; give it your love so it may love you well.

Jacques Bénigne Bossuet, Bishop of Meaux, (1627-1704)

The gifts of the Holy Spirit and the charisms

In spiritual theology it is taught that a person passes, at this stage of the spiritual life, from the active phase of the virtues to the (relatively) passive phase of life according to the gifts of the Holy Spirit. In general, this is true, though it needs to be added both that the virtues are never fully perfect, and that the gifts of the Holy Spirit make their appearance at earlier stages.

The moral virtues are aspects of our psychology which we provide ourselves with by dint of effort and repetition, although God is present in the effort. The gifts of the Holy Spirit are purely divine gift, without our deserving them or producing them by our efforts. To receive them it is enough to be attentive and ready to live them. They constitute as it were a new mode of the divine presence in the soul. They are given at the level of the 'deep self', and from there they spread out to the other zones of our being, which they take over little by little – not indeed without more or less conscious resistance on our part, as we shall see later on. The gifts of the Holy Spirit make a person very supple and allow him or her to obey without hesitation the inspirations of God. Traditionally, from the Old Testament, there are seven. Each of them brings a virtue to perfection and carries it far beyond what we could achieve by our own effort. The gifts of the Holy Spirit are not just 'presents', but the very being of God's own self, given to us. They are given to us along with charity, with love.

The gift of fear inspires in us a good attitude regarding God, that is to say, the proper respect that is his due. Fear does not mean being frightened, but the respect of a child who is careful not to offend our heavenly Father, whose greatness and whose closeness to us we know. This gift perfects the two virtues of hope and of temperance.

Correspondingly, the gift of piety leads us to have a tender love for God our Father, and to pray to him with confidence. It perfects justice.

The gift of fortitude, which of course perfects the virtue of fortitude, raises us gradually above all fear of the world and enables us to do what God asks of us without taking any account of obstacles.

The gift of understanding perfects the virtue of faith and leads us into the deep understanding of the truths of faith, beyond all reasoning. It is given even to those who are not highly cultured, and leads to the real spirit of childhood.

The gift of knowledge also perfects the virtue of faith. It enables one to see the world with the eye of God. Provided with this gift, a Christian certainly does not know everything, but at least is not in error about the general truth of things, seeing black as black and white as white.

The gift of counsel perfects the virtue of prudence. It enables people to find their way through life with confidence, according to what is good for us and for others, in the light of the will of God.

The gift of wisdom is the great contemplative gift. It perfects the virtue of charity, by giving us a sense of and a taste for God. It leads us more and more into contemplation. It is the most necessary quality for any soul that loves and desires God.

The gifts of the Holy Spirit, which are rooted in the sacrament of baptism, are given in the fullest way in confirmation. But the out-pouring of the Spirit [in daily life] activates them, makes them operative, and gives them new power, relevance and visibility. The results of the meeting with God, peace, joy, love, patience, goodness, faithfulness, gentleness and the rest, all derive from the presence in the soul of these gifts of the Spirit, and are described by St Paul as 'the fruits of the spirit'. (Gal 5:22f)

Ordinarily, the active presence of the Holy Spirit in the soul is accompanied by the charisms. These are, as we have seen, already to be found in the earlier Dwelling-places, but normally they are more powerfully present in the Fourth, because the soul is more disposed to receive them and to put them to work with fewer hindrances, in the service of the church and society. Certain charisms take on a highly spiritual form, in the case of the charisms often found in the primitive church, several times listed by St Paul. Such charisms are also found nowadays in the Charismatic Renewal: singing in tongues, charisms of text, of prophecy and of words of knowledge. Other charisms, like those of singing, of guidance of assemblies, of government, of teaching, and of discernment, which seem less spectacular, are equally important.

If God has once more given all these charisms to his church, it is not without reason. He wants Christians to be endowed with new strength and greater certitude in face of a society that is often hostile, so as to evangelise it. Once charisms have been discerned, they should be recognised, promoted and utilised. However, it is important not to confuse the gifts of the Holy Spirit with the charisms. The gifts of the Holy Spirit go much further and deeper. As the Congregation for the Doctrine of the Faith has said: 'The gifts of the Holy Spirit radiate charity like the light of the sun to sanctify the ones who possess them. The charisms are like mirrors which reflect that light to others.' A spiritual life based solely on the charisms would be in danger of lacking depth, however spectacular and gratifying for all concerned it might be. If the charisms came to an end – as could happen, if only so that God might help someone to grow in humility – what then would remain of the spiritual life?

To conclude, the spiritual life involves a great deal of experience. But it is more than experience, because the presence of God is always more than what he shows us of himself. So it is necessary to take account of experience, but not to make too much of what may be particularly spectacular. The essential point of spirituality is the growth of charity. That is why it is also necessary to avoid judging the interior lives of others. Some people are not good at describing themselves. I am sure there are many people of whom nobody takes any notice but who will turn out to be among the highest in the kingdom of God.

THE FIFTH DWELLING-PLACES: THE SOUL FIRMLY ESTABLISHED IN GOD

On one occasion, a Carmelite I was talking with drew my attention to the importance of the Fifth Dwelling-places. According to her, many souls were at this stage without knowing it (and worse, without their spiritual guides knowing it). Thus, they were deprived of the encouragement and help they needed. I later came to realise that there was truth in this suggestion.

What are the Fifth Dwelling-places?
Entry into the Fourth Dwelling-places *constitutes a shock* for those who want to live the spiritual life. It amounts to a real passage from one world to another. Then gradually, after (or even in the middle of) the trials we shall consider later, the soul enters into a more constant union with God in the very centre of its being. God establishes himself in the soul, and makes his dwelling there. He comes to be more intimate to us than we are to ourselves. For all that, we are not dispossessed or driven out of our own souls. We feel better than ever, and the personality reveals itself to itself with much greater authenticity and simplicity than before. The person becomes more simple, many wounds heal, he or she feels truly himself or herself. At times we may even feel that we have been established at the Heart of God. There is no opposition between these two impressions.

In this stage, it is not difficult to recall to mind the presence of God 'in the heaven of the soul', as Blessed Elizabeth of the Trinity used to say. The soul has been conquered by God, and its higher part penetrated by his presence. Regarding the rest of the soul, one is not so clear where God is or what he is doing there, because one knows how vast the soul is and how part of it can escape one's knowledge, but that does not matter. One can let oneself be.

There is no question here of doing any particular thing. It is not a decision to be taken. Things are just so. It is a question of a 'state' rather than an action, and an entirely passive state. It involves very little thinking, especially in prayer. Teresa of Avila speaks of 'this soul that God has made quite stupid'. 'The mind would like to occupy itself wholly in understanding something of what it feels, and, as it has not the strength to do this, it becomes so dumbfounded that, even if any consciousness remains to it, neither hands nor feet can move.'[8] One of my friends, an academic, whose intelligence is always alert, used to say that he only needed to enter a church for his intelligence to stop at once. He found himself in the presence of God and had no longer been capable, for years, of conducting any reasoning about God. God was there, with him, and that was all.

Naturally, people in this Dwelling-place could, in prayer, try to reason and to meditate on the Word of God, and so on. But one is only taking up a position and does not get anywhere. One could spend a whole hour getting one's thoughts in order, to no good effect. The only thing to do is to accept this loss of thought and sentiment. At the beginning, this leaves one uneasy. One wonders if one's intelligence level has dropped. But as one sees how the work of God is showing itself in one's life as a whole, one finishes by peacefully accepting things as they are and remaining there, with the Lord, in his gentle and powerful presence. This is called the prayer of union or of simplicity. The Curé of Ars, as the well-known story has it, saw a country-man going to the church and staying motionless gazing at the Blessed Sacrament. One day, he asked the man what happened between

God and him like that: the country-man replied simply, 'He looks at me and I look at him.' That is more or less what happens. If you have a sense of humour, once you are over your surprise, it is an amusing situation: you feel a bit of a fool and you see that this in no way hinders the action of God. Fundamentally, such stupidity does not matter. However, it would be better to keep observations like this to oneself for fear of being misunderstood and giving unnecessary scandal.

Bossuet has given a good account of this prayer. His description applies also to the Fourth Dwelling-places. Take note of the passivity that pervades it.

> *A Description of Simple Prayer*
> We must grow accustomed to nourishing our soul on a simple and loving look at God and at Jesus Christ Our Lord; and, for that purpose, we must move gently away from reasoning, discursiveness and a multitude of sentiments, so as to remain in simplicity, respect and attention, and thus to approach closer and closer to God, our first beginning and our last end ... Mediation is excellent at its time, and very useful at the beginning of the spiritual life; but we must not stop at it, because the soul, by faithfully mortifying and recollecting itself ordinarily receives a prayer that is more pure and intimate that can be called that of simplicity, which consists in a simple loving look, or gaze or act of noticing of oneself, of God as he is in himself, or of one of his mysteries, or another of the truths of Christianity. The soul by leaving reasoning aside is thus using a gentle contemplation that keeps it peaceful, attentive and open to the divine operations and impressions that the Holy Spirit sends; the soul thus does little and receives much; its work is easy and fruitful; and, as it approaches closer to the source of all light, of all grace and of all virtue, it comes to be correspondingly filled with these qualities.
> *Jacques Bénigne Bossuet, Bishop of Meaux, 1627-1704*

Knowledge of the supernatural world
Strangely, while the intelligence works very little, one becomes more and more exact in matters of faith and of the life with God. This is the effect of the gift of understanding that freely reveals itself. One does not seek to keep to oneself what one comes to understand. Intellectual pride has been reduced, thanks to the spiritual trials one has undergone. The spiritual conscience is very much alive. One can see in one's own soul and in those of others many things that one would never have suspected before. One 'feels' very clearly the presence of God and the direction of his action, especially in the case of other people, and sees where he is and what he does. One becomes capable of helping souls in a way that is more appropriate and more profound, distinguishing human half-truths, any action there may be of the devil, and the invitations of God. One knows that what one experiences is true, and has no doubt. One moves with relative ease in this universe, which is new though already one has been involved in it: we have been visitors there before, but now it is where we reside.

This simplicity of intelligence facilitates the guidance of God when that is needed. It can also speak by way of interior words, direct suggestions, words of knowledge. One knows very well what is appropriate and is rarely if ever mistaken. God gives this taste for truth, allied to his presence. Years later, these interior words will have the same effect as if one had only just received them. This is something we shall return to.

Another aspect of this familiarity with heaven is often the existence of communication with the Virgin Mary, and certain saints and angels. There was already something of that in the person's life, but it now becomes more marked. The presence and the influence of the saints begins to be 'felt' differently from that of God, but clearly nonetheless. This is a gift from God to help us advance more quickly.

It would be possible in connection with the Fifth, as with the Fourth, Dwelling-places, to fear illuminism, illusion and quietism. One could think of oneself as having 'arrived'. Only good spiritual accompaniment from an experienced person permits us to see how things really are. It is to be noted also that real life with God is always marked by visible progress in humility, charity, the sense of service, and love of the church. Even a spiritual guide who does not have experience of mystical states can recognise these. Everyone remains weak and sinful. If someone used charisms or mystical experiences as an argument dispensing him or her from charity, it would be a very bad sign. Illusion and the demon would be lying in wait.

'HE MUST INCREASE AND I MUST DECREASE': THE RE-EDUCATION OF THE HUMAN PERSON

Why undergo 're-education'?
For God to be able to establish himself in a soul, it must be supple. Now that is not something the soul naturally is. Certainly, at this stage of the interior life, a person will no longer want to lead a life of sin, and will have left behind at least the greater habitual sins. What remain are pride, sensuality, egotism, and so on, at the involuntary level. As soon as one can, one corrects them, and does not hesitate to ask pardon from God and others. In the Fifth Dwelling-place one is already well advanced in these ways.

Nevertheless, there remain, as we said earlier, traces of original sin. Human nature is wounded by this sin. It was, as it were, in a vertical position, but now is off centre. It needs to be straightened up in order to live well with God. We may try to achieve that ourselves, but our scope for action on ourselves is limited. A good part of our unconscious is unknown to us. For this reason, God, as a good teacher and a loving Father, accomplishes in us the work of 'restoration'. He does not do this until we are ready for it, and this is why the 'nights', as they are called, do not come until these stages of the spiritual life. This does not mean that there are no trials and difficulties earlier, but that they are not on the same scale. At this stage the love of God is so strong in our hearts that we are capable of acts of courage which we could not have produced before. We are ready to decrease in order that God may increase in us, as St John the Baptist said regarding Jesus. (Jn 3:30) St Teresa of Avila remarks that the soul in the Fifth Dwelling-places is like a silk-worm that must die to itself in order to become a beautiful white butterfly.

Traditionally a distinction is made between two 'nights': the 'night of the senses' and 'the night of the spirit', which normally comes later. They are very different from earlier trials in the sense that they are 'passive'. In the first part of the spiritual life, there is the spiritual combat. In it, one struggles with oneself, and tries to dominate and limit one's evil tendencies, in which, with the grace of God, one has had some success. If one had not, that would either show a psychological illness or a failure to make real progress in the life with God. At the stage we are concerned with now, the work of God is being done, as it were, without us. We are going to be acted upon. All we can do is consent. It is a painful matter, because St Thomas Aquinas rightly says that it takes more courage to resist than to attack. We are rendered incapable of our own interior purification, which is no small matter.

> *From the prophet Isaiah*
> Seek the Lord while he may be found, call upon him while he is near. For your thoughts are not my thoughts, and my ways are not your ways, says the Lord. For as the heavens are higher than the earth, so are my ways higher than your ways, and my thoughts than your thoughts.
> (Is 55:6, 8f)

The night of the senses
The expression 'night of the senses' should not be taken too literally, because it covers much more than the senses strictly understood. What it does chiefly cover is the zone of the sensibility. But it concerns also the body and is not without an impact on the intelligence. Its goal is to put in order the whole domain of feeling and action, so that we may not be permanently overwhelmed by our impressions and personal projects, and can permit God to work in us without interference.

It should be noted that common sense requires the purification of this domain. The human sensibility is extraordinarily powerful. Take for example the areas of love or of dominance. We can be completely pervaded, dominated, led, or inspired by the memory of what we have lived through and by what we are actually experiencing at any given time. It is an inexhaustible source of inspiration for novelists and film-makers. If for no other reason than that, it is vital to put the sensibility in order.

But there is more: the felt presence of God in us is of far greater power. Certain unusual spiritual phenomena show that well. The body and the sensibility are raised up by the grace of God and transported to an astonishing extent. Even if we do not live through such phenomena ourselves, all those in whom God acts find their sensibility affected in the deepest and strongest way. It is impossible for God to act in the 'deep self' without affecting the other zones of being. Now, if I receive God into my subjectivity, in the first instance, (that is to say, am more aware of myself receiving than of God coming to me), then it is not he who is going to live in me, it is I who am going to indulge the sensations that he gives me, and these are not trivial sensations. I am going to close in on myself instead of opening myself out, and will very quickly create for myself a false mysticism dominated by affectivity. I am going to appropriate the graces of God for myself and insert them into my own system of existence. So it is absolutely necessary for the sensibility to be purified in depth, so that I can receive the presence of God into myself with the child's purity of soul.

As a rule, the night of the senses takes place in the ordinary circumstances of life. It goes like this: formerly, generally speaking, everything was doing well. Then it all falls apart. Everyone builds his or her life on a certain number of elements that for them are fundamental: safe employment, a secure relation with one's family or affective circle, a plan of life in one direction or another, good health, a strong relationship with God in prayer. It is like a house built piece by piece on stilts. And then it is all swept away or at least in danger of being.

For example: a young Catholic girl has a precise project of life in which God has an important place. She does well in her studies and it is preparing for a professional role that will later be of benefit to society. Her health has always been good and God has really shown her that he loves her personally. Everything is going well and fitting well together. But then her studies become difficult and she asks herself whether, despite all her efforts, she can make the grade. And suddenly her health is in danger. God himself withdraws from her in prayer, and she no longer feels anything at all. In this context, what is to become of her life plan? What can she depend on? Where to go? What is the key? Nothing is clear any more. What to do?

Again, a Christian teacher is highly reputed for his work and has a good plan for a thesis. He belongs to a community that supports him, even if there are some problems within it. His health is good. But suddenly serious difficulties arise with his thesis supervisor and his progress in the university seems to be in doubt. Yet, that is the place where he has invested many years of service of God and people, and nothing else has any interest for him. His spiritual life undergoes a sudden thrust forward owing to a personal encounter with Jesus which renews his spiritual strength, but his community is very traditional in outlook and does not understand this development, so that he can no longer feel at home in it. The exterior and interior tension is so great that he begins to feel he cannot physically hold out. How is he to decide? What is the way out?

Examples could be multiplied. What they have in common is that people are 'de-programmed'. They are no longer in control of their own existence. They come under attack, when all is going well. The horizon of life seems to disappear. The 'system of life' is profoundly affected. It is a time of great suffering. What has occurred is not an injury that will heal, but something quite different, something profoundly shattering. All the more so because it is clear that one cannot deal with it by oneself. All efforts to progress, and all plans, come to little or nothing. It seems as if life itself is going to stop, even though everything was fine a short time before. But now what does all past experience count for? Where now is the divine tenderness, so recently felt?

Reading spiritual works that describe the phenomenon can help, but does not solve the problem. The only thing to do is to understand that God has taken control of operations. I gave myself to him, and did so in the light. Now, I am caught. I have reached stage two of my giving, the passive phase. It is one thing to give oneself. That affords considerable satisfaction. It is another thing to be accepted, taken, caught. That feels completely different. People not ready for it wonder how long they can endure this alienation from all that was familiar.

Fortunately, God is very perceptive and very skilful: he does not try us beyond our strength. There is suffering, but not collapse. Every day, God sends help as needed, sometimes only exactly what is needed to survive that day. If life becomes too difficult, God sends a rescuer. After some time, one is amazed to find that one has not sunk without trace. It is rather like Peter walking on the water: it is rather foolish, but it enables one to get by.

On the whole, those around us do not understand what is happening and are not much help. They appeal to inappropriate criteria of judgement and make unworkable suggestions. But God sends the needed guardian angels. Sometimes these are people who momentarily cross our path. Sometimes they are people we already knew, but whose role in our lives changes, at least for a time. Our spiritual guides in these circumstances need to be people of experience, discernment, prayer and calmness of outlook. They must be close to those who are suffering without being drawn into their anguish. The night of the senses is a school of courage and of confidence for everyone.

In this night, at least some lights are visible – there are some indicators of which way to turn. The only way out is for one to agree to let things be, to consent, to abandon oneself. So, what to do? Basically, nothing. Just live. Live day by day, doing one's work as well as can be, praying as well and as faithfully as possible, even if that means feeling nothing, loving the best one can, putting up with oneself as little badly as possible. It is not the time of life for being at one's best. On the contrary, one hopes just to survive. Any progress is microscopic, or so it seems.

What is actually happening is that God is making us live in a school of abandonment. That is not something we are programmed for. We are active people. Agreeing just to let oneself be is like a major adventure. It is as well that the presence of the Holy Spirit in the centre of the soul is very strong, otherwise we would resume our independence and turn our back on God. Unfortunately this sometimes does happen. God then terminates the trial, the person reverts to 'normality', but makes no further progress in the spiritual life: that could only have happened by a radical renewal of the senses.

The night of the senses lasts some months or some years, depending on what God's plans are for the person, and his or her capacity to endure. It can begin and end either gradually or suddenly. It is more or less violent. It is a single blow or has several phases. In any case, there will always be some recurrences.

The night of the senses is a blessing from God in a person's life. Naturally, it is only afterwards that becomes clear. The suffering is extreme, but beyond that a new life begins. The Holy Spirit takes us over. Intimacy with God is much greater; it is even greater than it feels. One becomes pliable and ready to do what God wants. It is rather as if God were a hand and we his glove. The glove is stiff and ill-fitting, but God wears it in. The glove 'suffers' while that is happening, but when it has become flexible it follows the movement of the hand without difficulty or resistance. When it is all over, we will thank God sincerely, and would not have foregone the experience for anything. What is more, we will also have deep compassion for others who are in the night of the senses, and desire to be of whatever help one can to them.

PRAYERS IN THE NIGHT

Let nothing trouble you
Let nothing trouble you
Let nothing affright you
All things pass away
God does not change.
Patience obtains

all that it asks for.
He who has God
finds he has all things.
God alone suffices.
St Teresa of Avila

My Father, I abandon myself to you
My Father, I abandon myself to you; do as you please with me. Whatever you do with me, I thank you. I am ready for everything, I accept everything. So long as your will is done in me, and in all your creatures, I desire nothing else, my God. I place my soul in your hands; I give it to you with all the love of my heart, because I love you, and because giving myself is a necessity of love to me, to place myself in your hands without restraint, and with infinite confidence, for you are my Father.
Fr Charles de Foucauld (1858-1916)

I do not know what to ask of you
O Lord, I do not know what to ask of you. You alone know my real needs. You love me more than I could love myself. I dare not ask you for either cross or consolation. I can only wait on you.

My heart is open to you. Come to me and help my by your mercy. Strike me and heal me. Throw me on the ground and raise me up.

In silence I praise your unfathomable plans. I give myself in sacrifice to you. I place all my confidence in you. I have no other desire than to accomplish your will.

Teach me to pray, and pray in me yourself.
Archbishop Anthony Bloom (1914-2003)

Mary and the night
In general the night of the senses will pass much more quickly if we know how to place ourselves in Mary's hands. Basically, we do not know how to guide ourselves, we do not know where our

soul is in relation to the night, and the best of guides are very limited. But the Lord has given us a mother to look after her helpless children. Why not hand over purely and simply to her the conduct of our interior life?

If we do that, we are not asking her just for help. In my view, we should go further: it is necessary once and for all to hand ourselves over entirely to her and to leave in her hands the very conduct of our life – to hand over and never to ask back. If we hold this course, nothing will ever stop us.

Read the prayer that follows, which is by St Louis-Marie Grignion de Montfort. Do not force yourself: allow it to attract you, if it does. If you cannot say the prayer, there is no need to. But if, after you have prayed it, you are able to enter into this spirituality, you will find it changing your life.

> *Consecration to Mary*
> I choose you today, O Mary, in the presence of all the heavenly Court, as my Mother and my Queen. I deliver and consecrate to you, in full submission and love, my body and my soul, my possessions interior and exterior, even the value of my good actions, past, present and future, leaving to you the entire and full right to dispose of me and of all that belongs to me, with no exception, according to your good pleasure, to the greatest glory of God, in time and in eternity.

*

In all that we have just described, there is only one thing of importance, and that is love. Now, God *is* love. It is not that God has love, but *he is* love. So the presence of God in the soul is not something that comes from God, like a liquid that can be poured from one vessel to another: it is God himself who comes to us and communicates his love to us in perpetuity. To experience the world on the basis of love and in love is an incredible restructuring of the human being. It turns existence on its head. It is no exaggeration to say that human life then becomes utterly superb.

CHAPTER FIVE

Life of union with God

Although the life of human beings with God in the Fifth Dwelling-places is superb, God does not want it to remain at that level. God desires in fact a far stronger union with the one whom he loves and who loves him. It is natural to speak of this greater union in terms of 'spiritual espousal' and 'spiritual marriage'.[1] I would not wish to oppose this tradition and particularly not the whole 'spousal mysticism'[2] which it expresses, but nevertheless I will not use this terminology. I have learnt from experience that it is little understood today. Though at times it comes naturally enough to women, it is difficult for men to feel comfortable with, in contemporary culture.[3] In any case, these words cover a range of different meanings. For example, a religious sister progressing from temporary vows to perpetual could have the sense of passing from 'engagement' to 'marriage' with Christ, but that is not exactly what we are considering. All in all, there are delicate questions of language here, which I wish to avoid, so as to engage with the underlying reality:[4] namely, that there is a stage when a person is not yet completely at one with God, when there is still a certain amount of what is purely human, even if also spiritual. For that reason it seems useful to me to retain a distinction between the Sixth and the Seventh Dwelling-places, that is to say, between a union with God that is not fully consummated, and one that is altogether more complete. What then happens in these Dwelling-places?

> *The experience of an early Cistercian monk*
> The person who enters more and more profoundly into the mystery of God finds first the gentleness of that encounter, then the delight, then the wonder, then the forgetfulness of self, and finally the union. He says first, 'I remember God',

> then 'I am loved', then 'I know God by experience', then 'my mind cannot grasp what is happening', and finally 'I belong to God entirely'.
>
> Guerric d'Igny (+1157)

The contemplation of God

The term 'contemplation' or 'contemplative life' is used to speak both of the spiritual life in general and of the life of certain religious orders like the Carmelites or the Benedictines. This is a wide sense of the word. Here I am using it in a narrower sense, in relation only to the spiritual life. It appears to me that at a certain point of this life there is a new shift, a 're-polarisation', if we may use this expression.

The contemplative life is one in which how one attends to God gives direction to everything else. It is not just a condition in which God is always present, but much more than that. At this stage one will say that 'God is everything', or 'God alone'. A person no longer lives in a 'God for me' attitude, but in the 'I for God' attitude. I would not wish to say that God takes the person over, because there is no question of depersonalisation. Quite the contrary, one is more oneself than ever before. But the union of the divine and the human will is much greater than it was, and the various zones of the being are much more 'divinised'. More and more, God being all that matters, the different aspects of life are seen and lived almost naturally in relation to him. The person no longer judges himself or herself by human criteria, such as social acceptance and the desire for status, recognition, or success, which all become less and less important. There is a transition from the level of 'doing' to that of 'being'. The person is even ready to abandon the most cherished projects if that is what God wants. Even the idea of the future becomes secondary. My future is life with God, and since God is here today, with me, in me, and I in him, today is my future. My future is in the Heart of God and I am in the Heart of God. Divine time with its new rhythm supersedes human time. Not that I leave the world or cease to be active or to love people in it. But the basis of my life begins to enter into eternity.

LIFE OF UNION WITH GOD

It is by a better knowledge of the Three Divine Persons that we enter more profoundly into contemplation, into the reconfiguring of our lives from the centre outwards.

> *O Blessed Trinity*
> May the grace of God inundate and penetrate you
> spreading through you like a river of peace.
> With its gentle flow may it cover you
> so that nothing of outside may touch you again.
> In this depth, this calm, this mystery,
> the Divinity will come to you.
> It is there I will celebrate with you in silence, my mother,
> adoring the Holy Trinity with you.
> Bl Elizabeth of the Trinity (1880-1906)

THE ENCOUNTER WITH THE 'THREE'

Living in a personal relationship with each of the Persons of the Trinity is something extraordinarily sublime. St Thomas Aquinas spoke of the 'divine manners', meaning by that the different ways of being of each of the Three Divine Persons. In the spiritual life we are called to experience these different relationships with the Father, the Son and the Holy Spirit.

The relationship with Jesus

In the Fourth and Fifth Dwelling-places there was no advancing without having 'met' Jesus. That encounter is overwhelming, because it involved discovering him and making his acquaintance exactly as the apostles did in their day. One did not know what he was like, and now one knows. One knows his way of acting and his temperament. Christ is full of burning love, he is demanding, but he is also very approachable, a real brother and friend, as sensitive as he is strong. This personal discovery of the goodness of Jesus, of his friendship for me, and his inexhaustible mercy for me, is totally irresistible.

But there is something even more irresistible: it is the discovery that Jesus needs me. True, as God, he does not need anything at all. But the Word chose to become a human being. A human being needs other people, is made to live in their company, is built up as a person with them and through them. Jesus needed Mary and Joseph for his personal growth. He needed the holy women who assisted him materially. But there is still more: he needed their friendship. At Gethsemane, Jesus was tested to the limit, to the point of losing the very meaning of his name (Jesus means 'God saves') and the value of his sacrifice. Why? Because, as he told St Margaret Mary Alacoque, the devil tempted him by saying that his sacrifice would achieve nothing. At that moment, Christ needed friends to help and console him. That was why he had brought Peter, James and John, his privileged friends, to keep him company. But they could not keep sleep at bay, and so they left Jesus alone in his terrible struggle without support or consolation, as he thought that human beings would always be tepid in the face of his burning love. Now, to understand Gethsemane properly it must be seen both as within time and as outside time: I am there too, like Peter, James and John. Jesus needs me, he needs my affectionate companionship, my support. I can either be lukewarm and indifferent, or I can be present and consoling, like a true friend. That is the profound message of the Heart of Jesus as he gave it at Paray-le-Monial.

It seems like folly to think that God's espousal of human nature goes as far as this, but it does. There is a real folly in the love of Jesus, which I am invited to enter into. One of the best aspects of contemporary spirituality has been the discovery, or rather the acceptance, of the sense of the vulnerability of God in Jesus Christ, of the divine pleading that makes of God, in a sense, a 'beggar seeking love'.

As time goes by, the person living the spiritual life discovers another thing about Jesus: his dimension as Son of the Father. Not alone is he my particular friend and my Saviour, he repeatedly says of himself that he is Son. The gospel of John says nothing else. Clearly the Son does not stop at himself, but wants to introduce people to the circle of an Other. He takes our hand to lead us further. Then one understands, and because one is in union with him, one experiences that the Son is all acceptance, all 'Yes' to the Father. Someone who is not yet interiorly detached cannot know what this permanent and absolute 'Yes' is. People like that are still in the 'no' or the 'maybe'. Only a fully established spiritual life can unite a person to Jesus enough for him or her to receive the grace of being permanently accepting of the Father. Our whole existence is, as it were, suspended from the Father, it is a never-ending and marvellous gift.

The relation to the Father
Astonishing though the relation to the Son is, the relation to the Father is just as powerful, to say the very least.[5]

The spontaneous image of God is as power, as a force. True, in the Christian life, we find that that is not quite exact. But what can be said of the overwhelming feeling experienced when someone sees that God is essentially Father? The encounter with the Father makes us realise the goodness of him who is the source of our being. We see that we have been created by pure goodness, that we are enveloped and penetrated by tenderness. The Father is far from invasive, and by no means over-reaches us. His sole desire is the happiness of his children, and he gives them day by day what they need, since he is constantly occupied with them.

I am well aware, while I writing this, that I am repeating what I said in the first part of this book. But here, I would wish to say that this is not just something to believe, but something to experience. Someone can be penetrated once and for all with the strong and tender goodness, gentle and sure, of our heavenly Father. It is possible for us to live, if God grants it, a life that is referred, instant by instant, to the gentle will of him who loves us to a depth and to a degree of which we have no idea. To become truly a child, to be in the arms of the Father, in a completely non-sentimental way, is an indescribable experience!

What one then finds is of the utmost importance. Our heavenly Father is the Creator and the Master of the universe. He is its King. I am his child, and therefore his heir. Already, whatever belongs to him is mine. One ultimately comes to realise that our relationship to the universe has changed, since the world is the wonderful garden of my Father. Given that, what could I lack? The words of Jesus on the subjects of filial confidence and the generosity of the Father take on a different dimension. Being poor is not something to fear, because the poor are kings. False wealth loses its attraction. Not that the universe is reduced to nothing, far from it. But that, according to our particular role and needs, all we need is given to us. We then see things according to their true value, admire their beauty, and are unceasingly grateful for them.

> *Father whose name is Mother*
>
> Father whose name is tenderness, Father whose name is youth, Father whose name is love.
>
> Father whose name is Father, and whose name is almost Mother, Father whose name is help.
>
> Father whose name is kindness, Father whose name is patience, Father whose name is pardon.
>
> Father whose name is caress, again whose name is tenderness, Father who call yourself infinitely good.
>
> O Father, to those who on the pretext that you are completely different, want your fatherhood to have no relation to ours, and who make of you what they would not want themselves to be, a fearsome judge, a Pharaoh, enable me, O Father, by means of human words tasting only of God, to make your true name known.
>
> François d'Espiney (1916-1935)

But there is yet more. If I am the child of the Father, I receive not alone his wealth, but something of his own heart. Now the Heart of the Father is precisely being Father. That means that God communicates to us sooner or later something of his Fatherhood. We in turn become fathers. In the Bible, God's attributes are feminine, and God's love is also compared to that of a mother. The two attitudes of fatherhood and motherhood come together here, as they do in the prayer given just above.

What we are concerned with here is not a superiority that

would involve domination. We are not the masters, still less the owners, of others. But we receive something of this sense of life and growth, of help and of need, of goodness and commitment for the future, that are found in the Heart of the Father. As Christ has told us, we do not have ourselves called 'father' in the sense of superiority but, just as Jesus himself has used the words, 'my daughter', 'the children', or as St Paul spoke of 'his children', we are fathers by and for love and service. This paternity is independent of physical generation, although it can go along with it. He can be found in celibates, or in childless couples. It is a great mystery to launch or to re-launch young people in their lives, or for that matter, grown men and women. It is an inescapable mystery for oneself in which one becomes involved bit by bit. Our Father in heaven gives all that he has and all that he is. In him, we are all called to the same thing. But, as in the case of the relationship with Jesus, it is not possible except for those who have already renounced themselves, to a great extent.

> *The experience of becoming a father*
> Becoming like the heavenly Father is not just an important aspect of the teaching of Jesus, it is the very heart of his message [...]
>
> The heart of the gospel message is this. The way in which human beings are called to love each other is God's own way of loving. We are called to love each other with the same generous and welcoming love that we see in the representation of the father in Rembrandt's painting [of the return of the Prodigal Son]. The compassion needed in our love cannot have any element of competition in it. It is an absolute compassion from which all trace of competition is excluded. It should be a radical love of one's enemies. If we wish not alone to be received by God but to welcome like God, we must become like the heavenly Father and see the world through his eyes [...]
>
> As the years go by, I discover how arduous and stimulating, but also how pleasing, is this growth in spiritual paternity.
> *Henry J. M. Nouwen (1932-1996)*

The relation to the Spirit
Just as the Son has already shown himself in the Fourth and Fifth Dwelling-places to be a person for us, so has the Holy Spirit. One has 'sensed' him, and knows who he is. One knows that one always lives in the Spirit, and that everything happens through him. His way of action has become familiar, free and disconcerting, sometimes full of tact, sometimes brilliant and full of power.

In the Sixth and Seventh Dwelling-places, the Holy Spirit leads us well beyond action. He introduces us into the very being of God and has us live something of the relation between the Father and the Son. Nothing we receive from the Father (all given love) or from the Son (all received love) would exist without the Holy Spirit (all exchanged love). It seems to me that the Holy Spirit is like the singing of this love, like the joy of this reciprocity of gift, like a permanent extolling of the glory of the Father and the Son. It is the Holy Spirit, I believe, who has us join in his own singing. He is the joy of the love of the divine Persons. He associates us with – no, rather, he introduces us into – his own praise. With him life becomes a constant song of joy and blessing.

Thus, life with the Three becomes 'a praising hymn of glory' as Bl Elizabeth of the Trinity puts it so well (borrowing from St Paul, Eph 1:6). The course of our life is thus penetrated to its very depths with a song that is not ours, a joy that comes from elsewhere and repeats on earth – very faintly – something of elsewhere.

By the Holy Spirit, the praise, beginning from the 'deep self', spreads into the intelligence, where it becomes admiration and affirmation, and then into the sensibility, which becomes more beautiful, more open, more confident, and sometimes even into the body, which becomes as it were more serene and luminous. It is then easier for us to speak of God, because one shows him not only by what one does, but also by what one is.

A Carthusian's words
This mutual inhabitation, this fusion, this 'amazing intimacy'

with the three Divine Persons: this is the higher goal that we must allow souls to glimpse even at the beginning of the spiritual life, for this is the desire and will of Our Lord. It is not enough to impel souls towards a heavenly ideal, it is necessary to have them enter into the kingdom of God, and understand that it is their heritage, already here and now: 'The kingdom of God is within you.' (Lk 17:21) Without this life of union with Our Lord, and this association with the Father and the Spirit that is its consequence, there is no depth of spiritual life, and no real spiritual fruitfulness.[6]

ENTRY INTO GOD'S FAMILY: THE SIXTH AND SEVENTH DWELLING-PLACES

The exchange of hearts

In the lives of a certain number of saints a very striking phenomenon occurs which is called 'the exchange of hearts'. Christ takes the heart of the saint, and gives them his own instead. From that moment there is total unity between them, and the thoughts that penetrate their hearts are those of the Heart of Jesus himself concerning his Father, in the Spirit, and concerning people.

There is here an expression of something that is given, in one form or another, to those whom God calls into the way of radical love. Marriage is a communication that ought to be complete between two people: 'They are not two, but one only', as if the same heart beat in their two breasts, with a total unity of will, of feeling and of thought. That is what the 'mystical marriage' seems to me to be like: a union of the heart of Jesus with each of us, which makes us enter into the very heart of the familial life of the Trinity: 'May the Holy Spirit lead us to the Word, may the Word lead us to the Father, and may we be consummated in the One, as was true of Christ', said Fr Vallée.

This, I believe, is how the expressions 'spousal' and 'marriage' should be understood in the spiritual context. They mean that something like a family life is established gradually, in an intimacy that is incredible and yet extremely simple, far beyond any mystical phenomena of whatever kind.

Life with the Three

What has happened in the preceding stages is that I have given myself to God and he has accepted me, bit by bit. Now, if I belong entirely to God, there is reciprocation. If God is everything for me, if I am his, then he also is mine. He has then brought me into his family. And to my mind it is perhaps there that the best definition of contemplation can be situated: now, I am part of the family, I have 'entered' the Trinitarian life and I am well aware of it. The 'Three' belong to me as I do to them, they live in me, but I live in them; they possess me, but I possess them also; I serve them, but they love me enough to give me their riches. We are in a state of familiarity. The relation is no longer that of respect and love only, but the love becomes kindness. This explains the familiarity of some saints with the Lord, like St Catherine of Sienna who used to say 'I want it!' with all her strength when she wished to obtain something of importance. God did not stand on ceremony, because everything was happening within the family circle. It is as if I were living now, in a barely conscious way (and an absolutely imperfect way) within the relations of the divine Persons among themselves. That is just what Blessed Elizabeth of the Trinity teaches.[7] It could seem quite mad, but still it is what happens! In any case, theologically, that makes sense: it is how we shall live in heaven. The astonishing thing is not the theory, but that it begins here on earth. And of course it is only a very small beginning. We are still at the start of a journey that will unfold only in the hereafter.

Some days before she died, Blessed Elizabeth, who was a Carmelite at Dijon, wrote: 'There above, in the house of love, I will actively think of you. What I will ask for you – and it will be the sign of my entry into heaven – is a grace of union, of intimacy with the Master. It is that, I confide to you, which has made of my life an anticipation of heaven: believing that a being called Love dwells in us at every moment of the day and of the night and that he asks us to live in companionship with him.' She also said: 'It is my Master who expresses this desire to me, my Master who wishes to live with me and the Father and his Spirit of love so that, in the expression of the beloved disciple, I may be 'associated' with them. "You are no longer guests or strangers, but already belong to the Household of God," says St Paul.[8] This is how I understand belonging to God's Household, it is living in the bosom of the tranquil Trinity, in my inner depths, and in this inviolable fortress of holy recollection of which St John of the Cross spoke.'

In the same perspective, she received from God the grace to write, on 21 November 1904, this marvellous prayer which is, all on its own, a treatise of spiritual theology and one of the most beautiful descriptions of the family union of a soul with its God:

> *O my God, Trinity whom I adore*
>
> O my God, Trinity whom I adore, help me to forget myself entirely, so that I may be established in you as still and as peaceful as if my soul were already in eternity. May nothing trouble my peace or make me leave you, O my Unchanging one, but may each minute carry me further into the depths of your Mystery. Give peace to my soul; make it your heaven, your beloved dwelling and your resting place. May I never leave you there alone but be wholly present, my faith wholly vigilant, wholly adoring, and wholly surrendered to your creative Action.
>
> O my beloved Christ, crucified by love, I wish to be a bride for your Heart; I wish to cover you with glory; I wish to love you … even unto death! But I feel my weakness, and I ask you to 'clothe me with yourself', to identify my soul with all the movements of your Soul, to overwhelm me, to possess me, to substitute yourself for me so that my life may be but a radiance of your Life. Come to me as Adorer, as Restorer, as Saviour, O Eternal Word, Word of my God, I want to spend my life in listening to you, to become wholly teachable that I may learn all from you. Then, through all nights, all voids, all helplessness, I want to gaze on you always and remain in your great light. O my beloved Star, so fascinate me that I may not withdraw from your radiance.
>
> O consuming Fire, Spirit of Love, 'come upon me', and

create in my soul a kind of incarnation of the Word: that I may be another humanity for him in which he can renew his whole Mystery. And you, O Father, bend lovingly over your poor little creature; 'cover her with your shadow', seeing in her only 'the Beloved in whom you are well pleased'.

O my Three, my all, my beatitude, infinite solitude, immensity in which I lose myself, I surrender myself to you as your pray. Bury yourself in me that I may bury myself in you until I depart to contemplate in your light the abyss of your greatness.[9]

THE ABANDONMENT OF THE 'OLD MAN'

In the New Testament, St Paul insists on the death of the 'old man' so as to put on the new man.[10] The 'new man', the renewed human being, is he or she who lives in the Trinity. But how can we put off our old selves so as to live in a different way? How can we effect such a change? How can we plunge down to our very depths?

The obstacles to grace
Who is called to live this life with the Trinity, to this contemplation of God already in this life? Each of us. Life with the Trinity is sanctity. The Second Vatican Council affirms, with all the authority needed, that every Christian is called, by his or her baptism, to become a saint. What we have described above is nothing else than the development of the baptismal life. To repeat, this holiness, and even this contemplation, I would hold is beyond what a person feels and especially what a person expresses.

Still, many people never arrive at the contemplative life. This is the case even in monasteries that people join for that sole purpose. St John of the Cross himself says so. It is possible to be a good Christian, a careful and hardworking religious, without going any further. Why is this? The great Jesuit theologian Joseph de Guibert wrote: 'Loving God, praising him,[11] tiring oneself out, even working oneself to death in his service, these are all things that attract religious people; but to die totally to oneself, obscurely in the silence of the soul, detaching oneself, letting oneself be purified by grace in the depth of one's being from whatever is not God's pure will, that is the inner holocaust from which the majority of souls recoil, the exact point where the road divides between a fervent life and a life of high sanctity.'[12] Going that far is exactly what the night of the spirit means.

The night of the spirit[13]
In the night of the senses, a person is deprived of his or her activity, capacity for work, and feelings. Then one knows that action depends on God alone. One is up against barriers that God has made for us to cross. There is a sense of dependence on him in the whole area of feeling and of action. The night of the spirit goes much further. It is oneself that has to be abandoned. The realisation is that one depends upon God for one's very existence. People always tend to fall back on themselves. In the night of the spirit, the very roots of life are exposed. As an engineer friend of mine puts it, with a touch of humour, 'In the First Dwelling-places, we are in the solid state; with the night of senses, we go into the liquid state; but with the night of the spirit, we are in the gaseous state.'[14]

The night of the spirit often touches the memory, our way of situating ourselves in relation to our past, our present and our future, our entire reference system. For example, there can be a complete loss of conscious memory of what God has done for us and of what we have done for others in the name of God. All that can vanish into a 'black hole'. The intelligence can be affected, at least the spiritual intelligence, and that precisely as regards consciousness of God's action. Pierre Goursat, the founder of the Emmanuel Community, who had a reputation for sanctity when he died, said that he was absolutely incapable of seeing what God could do in him and had lost most of his memory of God's action in his past. He lived in God just as in the present, in his hands, without being able to hold on to anything but him.

The purpose of this purification is to enable us realise the radical incapacity of being even a good Christian without the constant assistance of the Holy Spirit. That is why God permits the return of temptations that one had thought long over, and sometimes even serious sins. Spirits of impurity, pride, and blasphemy can attack the soul. It can lose the sense of faith, of hope and of charity. The things that most profoundly affect the soul are the inability to depend on God because one does not 'feel' him, no longer feeling God's protection, believing that his power is far away and that one is exposed to everything, thinking that there is no future, and lacking the power to love. A person is capable of confronting the most difficult things provided they are supported, especially if they know that God is with them. But if God is not there, if others move away, if we cannot even trust ourselves, what will become of us?

Thus very serious questions arise concerning oneself. The relation to oneself is affected: The questions are no longer, 'How can I act?', or 'What should I do in life?', but 'Who am I?' In this context, one can feel entirely lost. One's self-esteem drops, and it feels like plunging into an chasm. What is waiting for me there? Everything is so different, so much more terrible than what I experienced before. The core of one's personality is more or less in dispute. It is 'point zero'.

The trial is so intimate that it is not easy to find help. Advice does not go very far. The simple and trusting love of our friends, the consolation of a proffered hand, are often what enable us to hold on. Again, it is like Jesus in Gethsemane. At times we have need of being consoled ourselves, and those who do that best are not always conscious of what good they are doing.

Ultimately, one sees clearly that there is 'only God'. We are enabled to abandon our intelligence and our will, our memory and our plans, and beyond all that, our burdensome self. The 'deep self' is purified. Everything is simpler now. God is there and God loves me, I am there and I love God. We are Heart to heart, like Jesus and John. We are together and what more of it? Let him do with me what he pleases.

What remains is that one sees that God is not absent, has not left us, has not recoiled from our questions about ourselves and our misery. Better still, it is the light of God himself that burns in the depth of our being. That light introduces us thus to the new Wisdom of which we have already spoken.

> *Extracts from The Canticle of the Soul*
> *of St John of the Cross*
> O light who have guided me, O night more loveable than dawn, O night who have brought together lover and her well-beloved who has been transformed in him!
>
> On my breast adorned with flowers which I kept entirely for him alone, he rested asleep, and I caressed him, and with a fan of cedar I refreshed him.
>
> I stayed there and I forgot myself, my face towards the Well-Beloved. Everything ceased for me, and I abandoned myself to him. I confided all my cares to him, and forgot myself among the lilies.

The science of the Cross
When Jesus died on the cross, he did not do anything, he did not teach, but only offered. He was never greater, and his action was never more fruitful, than in this sacrifice. Neither have we ourselves ever been more fruitful than in this sacrifice. We do not have any desire to suffer, which is as it should be: I hugely distrust theories and pseudo-mystic declarations about suffering. But, being human beings, we suffer. We can pretend that it is otherwise, but in all truth, humanity suffers deeply. Moreover, even if we are not gravely ill, one day we shall die, and that will be a great suffering.

Jesus is very kind and sensitive, but he would have us discover the science of the cross. It consists in transforming the sufferings of this life into acts of sacrifice. This is not possible except through great union with Jesus and a relationship with the Father that shows that he accepts our offering. If we are united with Jesus, suffering is easier to bear, because the cross is always measured to fit our shoulders: 'My yoke is easy and my burden light.' Moreover, all that we experience becomes fruitful.

In the Christian life, there are several kinds of suffering. Some are linked to the structure of our being: when we have to put up with limitations and obstacles. Others are linked to the nights – that is almost the same. Others again are linked to the offering of oneself for the salvation of the world. With some people – sick people, old people, the dying – that can be God's direct call to them, and it can, as in the case of Marthe Robin (1902-1980) be a genuine vocation. For some religious orders, like the Passionists or those of a 'victim-based' spirituality, it is part of their charism. But every follower of Christ, in his or her own way, is called to discover this science of the cross, so as to contribute, in union with Jesus, to the salvation of the world.

Love and silence
In the state of constant union with God, of family life with him, the human being is completely engaged in love, and distances himself or herself from the pointless clamour of the world. Of course, there is no opting out of human life, people's various duties get fulfilled, sometimes even better than before, but in the depth of the soul there is the gentle and living silence of God's own self.

This presupposes a certain silence of heart. There is no question, it must be repeated, of distancing oneself from people, but of being a good distance from what is of no value for God's plan. A notable spiritual writer has written, 'Our heart is a temple bigger than that of Jerusalem. We should be alone in this temple with God and the Holy Virgin: because she does not disturb our solitude with God, but preserves it. There must be a great sense of calm: no noise, especially no debate [...] A certain capacity for exterior and interior silence is needed for souls to be able to recollect themselves and find each other in the heart of Jesus and Mary [...] Light can only reach peaceful souls: tranquillity is the first disposition needed for the depths of the soul to become transparent.'[15] And the Benedictine John of Fécamp (around 990-1078) wrote: 'To the soul that is holy and at peace, God shows himself without form, lets himself he heard without noise, perceived without movement, and touched without a body.'[16]

*

It requires no great insight to understand that we are here faced with, or rather in the midst of, an immense world. The further we advance, the more we feel its mystery; the more we speak of it, the more we are aware how far short our words fall; the more we have experience of it, the more we realise how little we have experienced of the things of God. As we progress towards the light, we sense more than ever deep night beyond the little day we can perceive.

But ultimately none of that is of any importance. God escapes all description. The itinerary he provides for us will never be fully comprehensible. Provided we are content to be children of God, provided we love him and love one another, what does our ignorance matter? We know enough to progress. It is said that St John, at the end of his life, could only ask his disciples to love. Was his life not focused on the essential point?

PART THREE

Towards a better understanding of the Spiritual Life

The spiritual life is not a journey that involves exactly the same itinerary for everyone. Different considerations apply.

The first is the call of God to the individual person, a call that may arise at the start of the journey or later, or a call that may be repeated at a later stage of life, perhaps quite a late stage. The latter is what is called 'a second call'.

All such calls take place within a more general call, which may perhaps mean adopting one or other type of spirituality. There are numerous spiritual families in the church, and it is as well to say something about some of them.

Another point is the way we deal with things that interfere with us or slow us down, especially the ways in which we have been wounded. This is something that has come to the fore again in recent times, and not surprisingly.

Finally, some consideration is needed of the unusual phenomena that occur at times. Granted that the spiritual life is not to be reduced to these phenomena, what purpose do they serve?

In this third section of the book, then, I wish to speak about elements that interact with the spiritual life at one or other of its stages, but which could not logically have been dealt with earlier. They can occur to some extent at any of the stages and have a different impact at different times.

I am going to develop the following five points:
– the variety of spiritual itineraries and the personal call;
– particular spiritualities;
– the 'second call';
– the wounded person;
– unusual occurrences in the spiritual life.

CHAPTER SIX

The variety of spiritual itineraries and the personal call

What we have written in the earlier chapters can only be useful for us if we live in great openness to the action of the Holy Spirit. The Spirit does not, of course, give people lessons to learn and tasks to perform, but deals with them as individual persons. People still differ very much from one another. God's plans for them, and through them for the world, are always original.

I have just written the words: 'God's plans'. The spiritual life is involved with the plans of God. What does God want for such and such a person? How is he or she to show people something of the love of God? The whole spiritual life is linked to this initial question.

THE UNIQUE VOCATION OF EVERY PERSON

Every human being has a particular mission
A human being does not progress satisfactorily in life without knowing who he or she is, what is within their power, and above all what he or she wants to do. In other words, everyone needs to know their own personal mission.

Ultimately, in the heart of each person, in their 'deep self', regardless of faith, there is as it were an intimate light that shows us what we are and what we are called to do, 'an interior monitor or sense, a conscience that provides us with knowledge of our own uniqueness', as Victor Frankl put it. It is a sort of inner call that requires total commitment. This mission is not an illusion or something that comes and goes: it is there. 'It is not something that can be radically changed in the course of life, although it can become more clear, more precise, wider or benefit more people.'[1]

If we do not respond to it, we will always have the obscure feeling of having spoilt our life. No doubt that is the source of much sorrow and many deviations. On the other hand, if we discover our mission – whether in our youth, or in the 'mid-life crisis' to which I shall return – our life is meaningful and dynamic. We will make something happen in the world, at least in a modest way. I know people who are not very prominent but who have described their lives to me as successful and happy because they have fulfilled their mission. A good example from history is St Monica, the mother of St Augustine, who passed on her last words to us. She left the world happy because she had accomplished her mission: helping her son to be converted. If I may be permitted, I may also mention my own father who gave me a mischievous and gentle wink as he set out on his final journey. He was delighted with what he had achieved, he had succeeded in his life, and he died happy.

This interior call, let us repeat, is to be lived in a flexible and free manner. Before going on to see how this works out in the spiritual life, I would like to allude to two attitudes very injurious to all interior life.

NOT BEING MOULDED: NOT BEING A MOLLUSC

The Jesuit, Father Jean Laplace, who was one of the great spiritual directors of recent times, pointed out one of the criticisms often made in former times of spiritual direction.[2] It did not take enough account of the Holy Spirit. It wanted to put souls into moulds, as it were. This will always be a danger. We work by means of models, not alone in the church but in civil society, and it cannot be otherwise. Some of these models are proposed by the church, in the persons of canonised saints or the charisms of recognised ecclesial movements. That is as it should be. The trouble is that sometimes a kind of tetanus emerges and things become rigid. You are expected to conform to an ideal projected on to you. I have noticed that this is a universal temptation, affecting people of completely different temperaments and movements that came into existence at very different times.

Now this cannot be right. The spiritual life of each person is unique. It progresses, it goes back, and at times it may take wrong turnings. Many things that people have within them go to make it more complex. 'A discernment that did not take account of the complexity of the desires at work in each of us, seems suspect to us today, and with good reason.'[3] It is not even useful, as a rule, to know exactly where anyone is in that regard. One can give general indications to help them move forward, without fixing them at this point or at that. So, I share the view of José Fernandez de Retana Arostogui when he says: 'It is a psychological error and not good sense to tell someone in which Dwelling-place they are, because until they are in the Seventh, that of transforming union, nobody can be sure of anything in the spiritual life. The Dwelling-places are neither static nor fixed achievements. That could be a very costly mistake for those being directed.'[4]

> *Remain prudent and unassuming*
> Who is the person who can judge another person? There can be rash judgements. People we despaired of can be converted and become excellent. People we expected great things of can fall suddenly and become very bad. Neither our fear nor our love is reliable.
> What anyone is today, they hardly know themselves. True, they know a little for today. What they will be tomorrow, nobody knows, not even themselves.
> *Saint Augustine (354-430)*

As against that, it would also be a serious mistake to be totally permissive and to abandon all spiritual rules, all plans of life, all consideration of the interior call, saying that it is up to everyone to construct their own life day by day, without any point of reference. That would be quite naïve, and would not lead very far in the interior life. It would mean being unstructured, subjective, sentimental, as it were like molluscs. This temptation too exists, has always existed and will always exist. The Holy Spirit does not always speak directly and at every moment to everyone, nor reinvent everything completely for me. If I think so, then I am in a worse situation than I realise. A body of spiritual directors who held this view would, to my mind, be a menace.

VARIETY OF SPIRITUAL ITINERARIES

What is God calling me to?

In order to make progress, an important thing is for the soul to know what God fundamentally wants from it. Certainly, there is the personal call I spoke of above. But can it be combined with another call that transcends it and comes from a greater distance? In other words, can we know something of God's will regarding our mission, our deep call? I am not speaking only about a vocation of a public kind, like the priesthood or the religious life. I am asking whether God can show us something of how he regards us personally? Does he want to tell us something of the secret name he has for each of us? If we know something of that, the spiritual life is greatly simplified, and we will progress within it more freely and decisively. The question always to ask is, 'What does God want of me, just as I am now?' It is the fundamental question of all spiritual life, while the question of where I am in my spiritual itinerary is useless or secondary. What does God ask of me?

The matter could be put differently. Jesus is infinitely rich in his personality and in the details of his saving mission. Every spiritual movement reflects an aspect of Jesus, but not all aspects. It is like a diamond of which we can see one facet, or several, but not all together. In this context, each individual also reflects something of Jesus. The beauty of the life with God is its immense variety. How can we know what we reflect of Jesus? What is the type of mission that he confides to us as part of his own? What type of relationship do we establish with him in the intimacy of our 'deep self'? If we know that, and are faithful to it, I think we shall progress well.

SOME EXAMPLES OF CALL

To make this clearer, I wish to give here a few examples of spiritual itineraries, out of the many that could be given.

Pierre-Bienvenu Noailles (1793-1861): discovering the secret of the Holy Family[5]

Pierre Noailles was born in Bordeaux just as the French Revolution was reaching its height. His family had been wealthy, but were ruined by the wars. Though baptised as a child, he did not receive a Catholic education, and was twenty before he made his first communion. This was a turning point in his life, when he discovered his talent for leadership and attracting followers.

He underwent a spiritual experience in a church at Bordeaux, the day before his first communion. Although at the time French imperial ambitions were at their height, and Napoleon had led his enormous army into Russia, '[Pierre] received from God such a grace that in a moment all the illusions of the world fell away for him, and the happiness of heaven filled him to such an extent that he seemed virtually to have left the world.' Three years later, when he had just reached Paris to begin studying law, he visited the famous seminary Church of Saint-Sulpice. There, before a statue of Our Lady, he felt a call to the priesthood which decided him to turn in that direction. He describes it simply: 'I heard her voice. She called me. She showed me the way. I understood everything.' From then on Our Lady was central to his life.

He entered the seminary as he decided, but his time there was hugely difficult. His health broke and he thought he was going to die. However, he survived and was able to continue his studies. Before long he experienced a spiritual attraction to the Holy Family of Jesus, Mary and Joseph, and came to see them as a reflection of the Three Divine Persons in their human lives. He realised that this vision of the Holy Family was something he was being commissioned to communicate to others, for the strengthening of family relationships.

This he began immediately to do on his return to Bordeaux as a priest in the 1820s. The Association of the Holy Family which he founded acquired a chapel, where a vision occurred some years later of Jesus in the eucharistic host, blessing the people.

Many people, even the church authorities, recognised this as clear proof that God was with the newly founded work, and that Fr Noailles was a divinely chosen instrument.

When he died nearly forty years later, his association comprised tens of thousands of members, and is recognised as being one of the more original and innovative foundations of the period. He displayed great skill, perseverance and spirit in promoting it, which brought him the reputation of a saint and a genius. He certainly was one of the major spiritual figures at a time when there were many. He never said a great deal about his own interior life, so that it is not easy to distinguish the stages of his spiritual growth. What can be said of him, however, is that a divine mission was given to him at a comparatively early age, that he recognised it at once, and that he spent his whole life fulfilling it.

Pierre Goursat (1914-1991): rebuilding the temple of the Lord[6]

The story of Pierre Goursat could hardly be more different, though he too made an important contribution to the renewal of the church, more than a century later.

His family originated in the south of France, but he was very much a Parisian. His father, like his even more famous uncle a well-known caricaturist, abandoned his wife and their two boys when they were very young. She was a woman of very deep faith, especially devoted to the Sacred Heart. But when Bernard, the younger boy, was only ten, he fell ill and died within a few hours. Pierre, who was then twelve, consoled himself by throwing himself into his school-work, and later into the world of art and study, specialising in Celtic antiquities. His faith he left far behind him.

Then at 19, he contracted tuberculosis, the great scourge of the time: he went to a sanatorium in the Alps for treatment. His girlfriend also caught the disease, but she died, leaving Pierre alone in the world, and raging against the world. Then for no apparent reason, he began to think of his brother, Bernard, and seemed to hear him saying, 'You do not bother to think of me any more, because your heart has grown hard.' Pierre went instantly on his knees beside the bed, praying and completely converted. He understood that he was called to the prayer of adoration, to lay celibacy, and to the work of communicating the gospel. That was in 1933.

Back in Paris, Pierre tried various means of communicating the gospel in different parts of the city. On the eve of the Second World War, some people who were urging Pierre to become a priest, introduced him to Cardinal Suhard, the Archbishop. He understood the lay character of Pierre's vocation, and together they committed themselves to the work of re-evangelising the de-Christianised world, and especially the de-Christianised city.

An incident in the closing year of the war opened a new dimension in Pierre's life. He was on the run from the occupying German army, and was on the point of being caught, when he distinctly heard an interior word coming from the Virgin Mary: 'Be at peace, you are safe.' Amazingly, his hiding place was not found. This experience created a Marian presence in his life, from which he drew new confidence, gentleness and a sense of the active presence of God.

After the war, Pierre returned to his life as a leading film critic, and of adoration. He lived very simply, prayed a lot, and was constantly in poor health. He founded a film magazine and edited it until his retirement in 1970. But that was by no means the end of his work for re-evangelisation. In fact the principal aspect of his mission had not yet become apparent.

This happened with the arrival of the Charismatic Renewal in France in 1972. Pierre discovered the Holy Spirit as a Person from his contact with the Renewal, and immediately became transformed with joy and hope regarding the future of the church. He set up in Paris, along with Martine Lafitte (today Martine Catta) one of the very first charismatic prayer groups in France. There were five members to begin with, and by the end of a year five hundred. It was from this group that the Emmanuel Community sprang. After initial hesitancy, which ended when he met the gifted mystic Marthe Robin (whom we shall consider next), he agreed to become the leader of the community. He held this position until his failing health made it impossible to continue, in 1985. For those twelve years he gave all he had to the community, teaching the first members to be attentive to the Spirit, helping them to avoid obstacles, discovering with them many forms of evangelisation, and above all establishing them in the practice of prayer.

Marthe Robin (1902-1981):
in the Heart of Jesus for a new Pentecost of love[7]
Marthe Robin is very well known as a major personality. And yet, what has been written about her has often remained at the level of the spectacular, and fails to reveal her character.

Marthe was born into a rural family, at Chateauneuf-de-Galure (Drôme) in the diocese of Valence. Their farm was in an isolated hill-side hamlet. She was a lively, intelligent and happy child, but at the age of sixteen she was struck by encephalitis, which grew steadily worse. At times the illness progressed, confining her to bed with terrible suffering, and at times it went into remission. She spent ten years fighting against this hopeless condition, and trying to make sense of her life. Her family could do little to help her, with hardly any education or money, no influential friends, and few comforts. It was a severe time of isolation, of deep boredom, of self-questioning. Later she would say how she wanted no one else to go through what she did: 'I fought with God ... I do not want any of you to fight with God.' Mercifully she had preserved her faith, and in in a hidden way, God was preparing her for a significant future.

A new situation began when a mission was preached in the parish in 1928. On that occasion she received an out-pouring of the Spirit and understood at once what her vocation was. A new life penetrated her body and her heart. Everything became clear and made sense: her hopelessness had become the place where God could act and bestow his grace. She received from the Heart of Jesus on the cross an understanding of her life as an invalid. United to the life of Christ, her life was to become fruitful for the church and for the world: 'The Sacred Heart of Jesus on the cross is the inviolable dwelling-place that I have chosen on earth'. Marthe made the choice of a life conformed to that of the crucified Jesus: a life based on resembling him, a life of loving him to the point of resembling him. In other words, by uniting herself to Jesus, she shared in the sufferings of Christ and Jesus shared in her sufferings. Her spiritual life no longer coexisted with her sickness, but became the heart of her sickness. Her acceptance of her sickness gave meaning to her suffering: 'After many years of anguish, after many physical and moral trials, I have dared, I have dared to choose Christ Jesus.' In accepting herself as someone who had to suffer by love, her life became very fruitful. Then Marthe understood that she had received a 'sacrificial vocation', that is, one of enduring sufferings out of love.

Her vocation was enhanced by a sense of the Virgin Mary's presence, which was so strong, tender and lasting that it made of Marthe Robin one of the great Marian souls of her time. She lived in a familiar relation with Mary, whom she called *'la maman,'* the dear mother. From childhood, Marthe had loved Mary with a childlike affection: for her she was always both mother and teacher. 'It is through Mary, with Mary and in Mary that I will go to Jesus and be entirely his,' she would say. She knew Our Lady so well that she was a source of inspiration and new insight for a number of theologians.

There then began a period of progress and discovery during which, amidst many difficulties, the spiritual personality of Marthe Robin gradually took shape. Jesus gradually brought under his influence all the zones of her being, giving a sense of his presence that remained with her day and night, to which was associated the deep action of the Virgin Mary. The result of this union was her receiving the stigmata in 1932, which conformed her still more to Jesus on the cross. From then on, every week she relived the passion of Christ. During the same period, she began to discover the Person of God the Father, and spoke especially of God as Father. She experienced the strength of the Father's love and constantly told those around her about it. In this, along with her Mariology, she provided significant support for the spirituality and the thinking of her time.

In 1933, the Lord revealed to her more of what her mission in the church was to be: the foundation of a new work 'for the extension of his kingdom in the whole church and for the regeneration of the entire world by a teaching that it would give, and whose supernatural and divine action would extend to the whole universe.' In other words, Marthe was called to bring into being, by the sacrifice of her sufferings, a community that would contribute to the renewal of the church and the world, and would later be called 'a new Pentecost of love'. A few years later, in 1936, she met Father Georges Finet, the priest who would help her set up 'Homes of Charity' (*Foyers de Charité*). This was a challenging undertaking, both humanly and spiritually.[8]

Her interior life continued to develop. Immediately after the Second World War, she underwent a long period of doubt and spiritual combat that brought her to a complete reassessment of herself. In 1948, she was at peace again. Physically, she continued to waste away, while growing in spiritual fruitfulness. When she died in 1981, the *Foyers* of Marthe Robin were to be found in many parts of the world.[9]

Marthe Robin's influence has been very great, corresponding to her mission. She received more than a hundred thousand guests in her little bedroom, and thousands of them found their lives transformed by her. She not only founded her *Foyers*, but renewed in people's minds the image of God as Father, encouraged the understanding of Mary's maternal mission in the world of today, assisted a great number of new communities, and re-launched the dynamic of evangelisation. In a world where people cannot see the point of suffering, Marthe gave meaning to her own by using it to share in the mystery of the death and resurrection of the Saviour of all mankind. When the religious history of our time comes to be written, she is likely to prove one of its most significant figures.

*

The three examples given above are of people who lived successful lives because they accepted from God the mission prepared for them. They set no limits to their acceptance, both in external action and, no less significantly, in prayer and the mystical life. Nevertheless, they should not be considered exceptional. Everybody has a similar call. The important thing is to ask God to make it clear in his own time, to sincerely want to know it and, in the meantime, to live a life of everyday kindness and availability.

CHAPTER SEVEN

The Different Spiritualities

God's call to a person often combines with another call: that of living in a particular spiritual family. There are in the church a significant number of different 'spiritualities'. It is not the same thing to be a Carmelite or a Benedictine or, for a lay-person, to be a member of a Rosary team or the Charismatic Renewal. Why is this?

Why are there particular spiritualities?
The reason is simple. Each spirituality expresses a particular aspect of the mystery of God, and enables people to live it out. It represents, as it were, a particular facet of a diamond. But none of them is the diamond itself. Or, to put it differently, each spirituality is like a particular gate leading into the world of God. The gates are all different, but they lead to the same place. The church is thus like a floral display which is beautiful because of its variety and its basic unity.

Each particular spirituality is centred on certain elements that are lived as the more important, motivating or driving themes from which all the rest derive. Some are based on the desire for the salvation of human beings, others on the love of the cross of Christ, others on trust in Mary, others on the urgency of Christian unity, others on the action of the Holy Spirit, others on commitment to the mystery of the church, and so on. Normally, each of them contains all the elements, but in different proportions. But, as in the case of a mixed drink, it is the proportion that makes the difference. For example, Mary will have first place in the spiritualities linked with St Louis-Marie Grignion de Montfort or Blessed Father Chaminade,[1] but she will have a different role in an ecumenical spirituality.

These different spiritualities are important for us. It is good to belong to a family which understands and sustains us. And seeing that others live the same ideals as we do, emphasise the same values, have the same spiritual tastes, we are encouraged, and feel ourselves better understood and guided. Sometimes though, we can, while having a dominant spiritual theme, receive something important from another spiritual group. It is necessary neither to confuse spiritualities nor to separate them rigidly as 'either ... or ...'. Often, God proceeds by way of 'both ... and ...' He makes different elements appear so as to bring them together and unite them when that suits his purpose.

There is no question here of discussing all spiritualities. That would require an entire historical treatise. But it may be worth considering a few examples, so as to encourage readers to identify their own spirituality, or rather to ask God to show it to them or confirm them in it. None of them is, in itself, better than any other. For people who are living as they should, every spirituality approved by the church leads to sanctity. The essential thing is to know which is the spirituality God wants me to have. Bickering between spiritualities is pointless. It savours of childishness and can produce results dangerous to the unity of the church.

SPIRITUALITY FOR LAY PEOPLE:
ST FRANCIS DE SALES AND HIS MOVEMENT[2]

When Vatican Two proclaimed the 'universal call to holiness' for all Christians, it was endorsing a very powerful movement already long established in the church. While the origins of this movement for lay holiness go back to the New Testament and the initial preaching of the faith, it is particularly associated with St Francis de Sales, whose key 'teach yourself holiness' book was published almost four hundred years ago. His book is called *The Introduction to the Devout Life*, has hardly been out of print since it first appeared, and has been translated into very many languages, including Irish a long time ago, and very recently, Swahili. It can be seen as the Catholic Church's adoption of a key idea of the Reformation, and for this reason constitutes a bridge uniting Christians together. To Francis de Sales perhaps more than anybody else we can credit the humane and joyful side of Catholicism as it has come down to the twenty-first century.

Francis belonged to the territory formerly known as Savoy, stretching from the east of modern France to Northern Italy. He was born in 1567 and his family planned a legal career for him. Initially he did study law, but then insisted on switching to the Catholic priesthood, in which he could see his own destiny. The church recognised his great qualities, and Pope Clement VIII appointed him Bishop of Geneva. He took up his residence at Annecy, because Geneva itself was a Calvinist stronghold. His early years as a priest and a bishop were spend in consolidating the faith of the people of the Cevennes mountains, and developing his ideas on holiness for laypeople.

One of his central convictions was that people respond better to 'a spoonful of honey than to a barrel of vinegar'. This led him to emphasise especially the emotional side of religion, and the gentler emotions such as patience, forgiveness and kindness. At the same time he does not conceal the need for great strength of character and a deep life of prayer in order to have a balanced emotional life. Equally, he recognises the truth of what a modern philosopher has said, that 'hearts are usually in much better shape if heads are less confused'. He considers that the greatest obstacles to true spirituality, after sin itself, are anxiety and sadness. And, that friendship and enjoyment are great aids to spirituality.

He held the view usually associated with Franciscan thinkers that God took the decision to be born as a human being from all eternity, before there was any question of original sin. In other words, God's pure love, rather than delivering the human race from evil, was the fundamental motive of the incarnation. Which, however, did not lead him to forget that the human race does very much need to be delivered from evil. Someone who begins to live a spiritual life must, he insists, first turn away from all serious sin and even lesser sins that are deliberate. In this, however, he sees no cause for sadness or regret, but only pure happiness and a sense of freedom. It is hardly surprising that the mentality of Francis de Sales spread rapidly throughout Europe.

However, the target group Francis aimed at was the less than 20% of the population who were literate. The Salesian lay spirituality movement needed to be harnessed to another force before it could have its full impact. This 'other force' was the growth in the movement of parish missions. Parish missions provided the illiterate and impoverished rural population of France with skilled teachers and talented preachers. As a result of their work, many hundreds of thousands of people began to experience the rich potential of their faith for the first time, and to make contact with the dawning of modern science. In particular, the missions given by St Vincent de Paul's Congregation of the Mission, based in St Lazare in Paris, were principally inspired by the methodology and vision of St Francis de Sales. Vincent's closest collaborator, St Louise de Marillac, was an outstanding example of the holiness and goodness to be found among those influenced by the writings of Francis. Her Daughters of Charity worked as parish nurses and teachers and brought practical holiness to the very roots of French society, particularly girls and women in the farms and villages. Simply lived Catholicism, which proved itself by caring for the worst off people in a district, began to flourish once more, guided by Vincent's motto, 'not merely charity, but organised charity'.

Progressively, the Salesian movement came to be institutionalised, not alone by Vincent de Paul and Louise de Marillac but by numerous others. Among the organised forms of practical lay spirituality were personal retreats, largely funded by generous donations from the wealthier sections of society, the parish missions already mentioned, and local confraternities of charity adapted to the needs of particular districts. Prison reform, famine relief and the care of refugees were among the other achievements of the Vincentian harnessing of the Salesian spirit.

There was also a much deeper side to Vincent de Paul's enhancement of Salesian spirituality: the contemplation of the life and person of Jesus Christ and modelling of one's whole life on him. Basically, this was what he learned from his spiritual mentor, Pierre de Bérulle, who used the radical biblical word 'adherence' for the personal attachment to Christ that he taught. Vincent went one step further than Bérulle by identifying the poor, sinners and un-believers as the ones whom Christ regards especially as his own in the world. For him, that was part of what is meant by saying, 'the Word became Flesh'. This vision, allied with his faith in Divine Providence, imparted powerful dynamism to Vincent's implementation of Salesian thought.

Unfortunately, the harsh interpretations of Christianity that were so opposed by St Francis de Sales and his followers re-asserted themselves as the years went by. In the France of the latter part of the seventeenth century Jansenism, a Catholic version of Puritanism, fused with the nationalistic version of religion known as Gallicanism. From New Testament times, the incompatibility of extreme nationalism [in its Jewish form] and Christianity had been clear. So it is not surprising that the Salesian movement lost its momentum by the beginning of the eighteenth century, which contributed to the political explosion of the French Revolution. The capacity of Catholic Christianity to hold society together dropped well below the level it attained during the lifetimes of Francis de Sales and Vincent de Paul. Matters were made worse by a significant split between the two foremost leaders of the French Church, Bossuet and Fenelon. They represented respectively an approach to religion that was overly simplified, and one that was too sophisticated, though the difference was perhaps more a clash of personalities than of principle.

However, the ideals of St Francis de Sales were not lost sight of completely, and in the aftermath of the Revolution (which spread throughout Europe) there was a restoration of Catholicism that consisted largely in a retrieval of Salesian values. The most prominent figures in this recovery were St John Bosco in northern Italy, founder of the Salesians, and later the French Carmelite sister, Thérèse Martin, better known as St Thérèse of Lisieux, whose 'little way' reproduced the spirituality of St Francis de Sales. The organisational genius and practicality of Vincent de Paul was mirrored in that of Frederic Ozanam and his co-founders of the Society of St Vincent de Paul. A significant lay spirituality emerged under their influence, and that of many others. It developed in quite different directions, not least the two kinds of spirituality we will next consider.

What has prevented the revitalised lay spirituality of recent times from reaching its full potential is the residue of atheism that the French Revolution, for all its positive achievements, left behind. God alone can transform the human heart that he alone created, and which he made his own in Jesus Christ.

THE SPIRITUALITY OF THE FOCOLARE MOVEMENT

The Focolare movement began in Italy, in the area of Trent, during the Second World War and has since spread through the whole world, and touches the lives of millions of people involved in it in different ways. The Focolare movement owes its origin to Chiara Lubich. Its spirituality can be summed up in some major themes:[3]

Jesus in our midst

The Focolare movement attaches great importance to the real, close and effective presence of Jesus in the world of human beings: *Gesù in mezzo*, as they say in Italian, 'Jesus in the midst'. Nothing is further from their thought than that he should be absent from the world he has created or the history of which he is the master. God is and remains a God who is close at hand, yesterday as today. And the 'place' where he reveals his presence in a privileged way is the eucharist. Consequently, the movement and its foundress have a great love for the eucharistic Jesus. The movement would be nothing without the daily or at least frequent communion of its members, because that is where the inexpressible spiritual transformation of the Christian united with the Saviour takes place:

> The Eucharist [...] brings about a union of the believer with God that goes much further than that resulting from

Baptism: it reaches a substantial assimilation. All of which of course needs to be understood in a way that respects the distance between Creator and creature. There is no physical fusion between the communicant and Christ, but a mystical assimilation, spiritual but nonetheless real, which allows us rightly to speak of a 'body'.[4]

But Jesus is present not only in the eucharist. He is also present in the brother or sister: 'Where two or three are gathered in my name, I am there in their midst.' (Mt 18:20) One of the strong points of the movement consists precisely in this discovery of God's love present in the midst of people who are assembled in his name. In consequence, fraternal love has been as it were rediscovered and has taken on new proportions. The charism of the love of people is thus one of the fundamental principles of Folocare: 'The love of others is the basic commandment. Any action becomes valuable if it is done in love. Without the love of others, everything we do is empty.'[5]

Unity

In addition to this, there is a mysterious consequence of this fraternal love. It may not remain at the level of surface relations, but must reach the depth of the person I am dealing with: in other words, 'make union' with him or her. Here we meet another foundational grace of the movement. Chiara Lubich is perfectly clear on the point:

> Our specific vocation is unity: it is the characteristic of the Focolare movement. Other concepts, other terms, can in one way or another express the different ways of going to God, all both divine and splendid ... But for us, the word that sums up our spirituality is unity. It contains in itself every other supernatural reality, every other commandment, every other religious attitude and practice.[6]

Clearly, this unity is basically the unity with Christ that is realised in the eucharist. But it is also unity with one's brothers and sisters, in which the presence of Christ is manifested:

If we are called to unity, our way to God passes through the brother or the sister. It is along this path, sometimes as obscure and dark as a tunnel, that one reaches the light. God asks us to follow this mysterious route in order to reach him.

People who follow the spirituality of Focolare are thus called to empty themselves of themselves, of their culture, their way of thinking, of their inner world, in order to become 'one' with the person they are speaking with. There is a real asceticism in this constant stripping away of oneself, but it is possible because in it Jesus himself grows in the heart of each one:

> Here is the cross we must choose every day, our cross *par excellence*. It is life for us and for all whom we love. If we take up this cross, it becomes Jesus in our midst.[7]

The abandoned Jesus

When Christ asks of us this degree of self-abandonment, he asks a great deal, but he can do so because it is what he himself has done. And this leads on to another, and largely unpublished, aspect of the spirituality and therefore the theology of the movement, that is, the intuition of 'Jesus abandoned'. It is a version and a deepening of the theology of the cross and its implications.

For Chiara Lubich, when Christ says on the cross, 'My God, My God, why have you abandoned me' (Mt 27:46) he reaches an almost unimaginable level of dereliction:

> The abandoned Jesus is the model of poverty in spirit. The poverty of the Son is such that God himself is absent for him, so to speak: he no longer perceives his presence. The abandoned Jesus is thus the model of renunciation and mortification. His suffering is not only physical – the torments of the cross – but his soul too lives its Calvary, because it has to forego the dearest reality of all, union with God. It is for Jesus neither more nor less than a total renunciation of his nature as God-man.[8]

As is quite clear, this text, which is only one of many, could be the subject of long discussion. It is profound in its implications. It is because the abandoned Jesus is united to the human race in the sacrament of the eucharist that he can ask of his brothers and sisters the abandonment that leads to unity.

There are innumerable consequences from this, which the movement has over time distilled into many undertakings in the direction of ecumenism, and 'economy of communion', and so on. It is these undertakings that have had such a transformative effect on thousands of people, and produced results for the church as a whole, that promise to be of benefit for future generations.

THE SPIRITUALITY OF THE EMMANUEL COMMUNITY

More recently, other forms of spirituality have appeared in the church, at once innovative and belonging to the great tradition of the church. One example is that of the Emmanuel Community.[9]

Its origins were in the Catholic Charismatic Renewal. In 1972, the Renewal, which began in the United States some years earlier, arrived in France. Some small prayer groups were set up. As we have seen, one of them began in Paris with Pierre Goursat, a retired film critic, and a young intern doctor, Martine Lafitte (now Catta) at its centre. Initially there were only five members, a year later five hundred, and other groups had been established. Quite soon, some members wanted to go further. It was this that led to the foundation of the Emmanuel Community, which spread rapidly. The community was officially recognised by the Holy See in 1998. In 2003, it had some six or seven thousand members, including sixty priests and a larger number of religious sisters, and it has spread to sixty-five countries. It is one of the charismatic communities that are most closely involved with the church. It has had many ecclesial missions entrusted to it, especially parishes, and it has itself developed many varied forms of evangelical activity.

The outpouring of the Spirit

The founder of the Emmanuel Community, Pierre Goursat (+1991) was fifty-eight when he encountered the Charismatic

Renewal, and he had been living the spiritual life for a long time. But when he received the prayer asking the Holy Spirit to renew him interiorly ('the outpouring of the Spirit'), he became as it were a new man. He had 'met' the Holy Spirit in person.

Hundreds of people subsequently shared this experience.[10] One day, whether as the result of lengthy and silent preparations, or unexpectedly, life changes. God becomes close. Jesus, who had been far away, comes to them suddenly. They then hand their lives over to God, and the Holy Spirit becomes their guide. This happens for people of all ages, all races, all states of life, and at all spiritual and human levels:

> The outpouring of the Spirit corresponds principally to an initiative of God through which he comes in a special way in order to show himself to people as someone living and approachable. Those who are renewed by this experience discover or rediscover the meaning of their baptism and confirmation. They respond to it by a conversion, a change in their lives that allows them, progressively, to put God at the centre of their being.[11]

The outpouring of the Spirit gives a particular 'colouration' to the spirituality of the Emmanuel Community. A positive sense of life emerges. People start believing in the future of mankind and of humanity, because God is present. They come to notice in every person what can be helped – become better. They are attentive to the gifts given by the Spirit and try, not only to put them into practice, but to consider the evangelisation of the world in terms of them. Moreover, if the Holy Spirit is active today, it is because he has something in store for the church. He wishes to renew her, to bring her to life again in the old Christian countries, and extend her to new. This is what produces a loving and optimistic vision of the church, far removed from the way the world speaks of her, and also the desire to love and serve her in every possible way. The outpouring of the Spirit is therefore the beginning of a journey: there is nothing less static than the spirituality of the Emmanuel Community.

A further consequence of this outpouring is praise. The Holy

Spirit is one of joy and light-heartedness: he is the Consoler. More than that, he opens people out to the praise that exists within the Trinity. Consequently, in the perspective of the Charismatic Renewal, the Emmanuel Community is a community of praise, gratitude, constant thanksgiving, in line with the Saviour's call to be 'always joyful [...] and to give thanks unceasingly to God'. (1 Thess 5:16-18) This praise takes many forms, from the resounding praise of great liturgies or assemblies of prayer to praise in the family circle. But it is not simply a practice: it is a way of life. The whole of existence is seen through a vision of praise, which becomes a form of prayer to which all Christians are called.

This praise does not make the members of the community isolate themselves. Quite the contrary, it makes them part of daily life. Emmanuel means 'God with us' in the ordinary tasks of life. It is God who has come in our flesh. As a result, the spiritual life is only going well and actively if it is worked out in a concrete, not to say a pragmatic way. The name God gave to the community signifies this call to incarnation, to the manifestation of God's presence in the midst of human life today.[12]

Adoration, Compassion, Evangelisation
Pierre Goursat was an adorer. 'He was consumed in adoration' as said of him at his funeral. He spent several hours daily before the Sacred Host, and he wanted all the members of the community to be first and above all adorers, that is to say men and women of contemplation before engaging in activity.

> 'The members of the Emmanuel Community engage to the greatest extent possible in a long period of daily adoration (where possible of the Blessed Sacrament).' (*Statutes*, n 15) By so doing they contemplate Christ present in his eucharist giving his life in love for the salvation of humanity. They carry out adoration not only for themselves, but for all humankind. They open their hearts to the infinite love of God so that this merciful love may be poured out in the world. They offer themselves to respond to the loving thirst Christ expressed on the cross. (Jn 19:28)

Adoring Jesus in the Sacred Host, participating in Mass, daily if possible, is not just carrying out acts of piety, but putting oneself more and more in an constant attitude and state of adoration. Adoration leads to a slow letting-go of oneself, to an increasing forgetfulness of one's personal projects, and to a consequent ever-strengthening presence of Jesus in one's soul. There is nothing humanly more 'useless' than adoration. Remaining in it, without doing anything, for long periods, can give the impression of wasting time that could be better employed. And yet it is the very source of life. If there is no adoration, activity is short-lived and superficial.

An important effect of adoration is the 'transfusion' of the sentiments of the Heart of Jesus himself. Mysteriously, gradually, one comes to think like him. And then one feels an immense compassion for the world, for people, and especially for their suffering. One becomes vulnerable, lowers one's guard. What comes to predominate, very soon, is sorrow at seeing people dying of hunger, not only physical, but still more, spiritual. It is the cry of St Dominic when he prayed in the night, a cry that Pierre Goursat often repeated: 'Lord my God, mercy! What will become of sinners?'

> The true compassion of Jesus is for the salvation of men and women created by God. To become a disciple of Emmanuel, is to be burning with the desire of contributing with him to the salvation of all humanity.[13]

It is therefore compassion, rooted in adoration, that gives birth to action. This takes the form of the desire to evangelise, to speak of Jesus, not to remain silent in the face of the greatest of poverties, that of the absence of God. It is impossible to remain passive, a bystander, while the world is losing its meaning, or to give up in the face of humanity's hunger, the hunger for God:

> The call of the Holy Father to new evangelisation only confirms the vocation of the Emmanuel Community to participate in the accomplishment of the church's mission in the world of today.[14]

THE DIFFERENT SPIRITUALITIES 143

This means that the Emmanuel Community is a community of missionaries. Under all its forms, in the family, at work, in the missions of the church or its own proper activities, the members of the Community are called to witness to God, equally in all the states of life (lay, clerical, consecrated), with the sensitivity that Mary gives and with the support of the suffering members of the community.

The Heart of Jesus
Strikingly, since 1975, the Emmanuel Community has found itself linked with Paray-le-Monial and the message of the Sacred Heart of Jesus, which was revealed there to St Margaret Mary between 1673 and 1675. Nothing suggested that a community based on the Charismatic Renewal would take up contact with a form of spirituality that seemed at that time to have run its course. However, the message of the Heart of Jesus had a decisive influence on the Community, which in turn has contributed to a renewal of the communication and presentation of the message.

The message of Paray is primarily linked to interiority. The heart is the centre of the human person, the place of the 'deep self'. To speak of the heart is to speak of a religion of the deepest parts of the person, of the spiritual part, rather than of a religion of doing. It is also to speak of a union between the Heart of God, that is to say, the secret of the Divine Being, and the heart of humankind: we are there in a spirituality of union. The message of Paray is then a message of love: 'See this Heart that has so loved people that it spared nothing, to the point of exhausting and consuming itself to testify to its love for them.' It is the whole gospel of John: God is love, the creation is a work of love, and the redemption attains in love to unimaginable heights. Paray is therefore a declaration of the love of God for the human race.

But there is in the message of the Heart of Jesus another dimension that the Emmanuel Community has discovered more and more: it is that love is not loved. Indeed, what Christ complained of to St Margaret Mary is the indifference of people, especially regarding his loving presence in the eucharist. And in Gethsemane, just when Christ most needed to be helped, even consoled, by his friends, this indifference becomes extreme. So, what the Emmanuel Community seeks is to console the Heart of Christ. Its members wish to approach him as his brothers, his sisters and his friends. It is astonishing to think that Christ wants to be in need of people to the point of calling for their friendship. And it is in adoration and in eucharistic communion that this friendship can best be manifested. So, the message of Paray is more relevant than ever, because the sentiments of the Heart of Jesus do not change and need to be communicated to all people in all generations.[15]

*

To repeat: the examples we have just given say only a little about the richness of the spiritual history of the church and the possibilities she offers to her children. Many spiritualities coexist together. It is not because some of them are older than others that they are less relevant. 'Living for ever', said Peter Van der Meer, 'The church shows herself in many forms. She lives in the silent prayer of the contemplative orders, she lives in the suffering of the poor as in the joy of giving, she lives also in the splendour of cathedrals or in the simplicity of small churches.' So it is also with the variety of forms of spirituality.

CHAPTER EIGHT

The 'Second Call'

Another aspect of our spiritual itinerary is what age we are. As is well known, the life of a human being does not move in a straight line. There is advancing and retreating. But there are also opportunities for 'a second chance' when our spiritual life can 'reconfigure' itself and take giant strides forward. This is certainly the case with what is called 'the mid-life crisis', which we are calling here 'the second call'.

The spiritual life and the ages of life
The spiritual life unfolds through the ages of life without being completely dependent on them: and older does not mean holier. Young people and children can be further advanced in the spiritual life that very old people. Nonetheless, when a person has made the choice of God, the Holy Spirit makes use of the time. It takes indeed a great deal of time, though how much depends on the individual, to become converted to a life of deep unity with God. St Teresa of Avila was right when she remarked: 'We are so slow to give God the absolute gift of ourselves that we never finish preparing ourselves for this grace.'[1]

The truth is that in every life there are transitions to be made – some painful – that touch us more or less deeply. At each of them, the Lord is present, and calls us to come closer to him. ('If I should walk in the valley of darkness, I shall not fear, you are there.' Ps 23:4) These transitions are the ordinary ones: the loss of a father or mother, or of some other dear one, professional inadequacy, the children leaving the home, retirement, and others. As human beings, they can shake us: as Christians, our relations with God can change; if we belong to a community or a movement, there are often challenges to be faced. These human crises are spiritual opportunities. They can lead to blocks and withdrawal, but they can also lead to a significant shift forward in life, a new departure, a second call. In the middle of life, we can change.

I do not intend here to speak of each of the ages of life.[2] I will speak only of one, because my experience is that it can be the decisive one for a new spiritual departure in one direction or another: and that is mid-life. I am not claiming to say anything original about it, but only to draw attention once more to its importance for the interior life.

In my approach, I shall rely on writers who have already made a study of the question. Initially, my source will be a contemporary founder, Father Voillaume, who wrote for the members of his community, the Little Brothers of Father de Foucauld,[3] and highlighted the phenomenon. I will here use his terminology and part of his analysis. I will add to it the reflections of a German Benedictine abbot, Dom Anselm Grün, who has written a book entitled *La crise du milieu de la vie*, 'The mid-life crisis'. He himself draws on illuminating texts from a medieval German mystic, Tauler (1300-1361) and the Viennese psychiatrist Carl Gustav Jung (1875-1961). All this indicates that the subject has attracted the attention of a number of people. I shall also add a reflection that was made in the setting of the Emmanuel Community by Louis-Gabriel and Omblyne de Jerphanion and myself.[4]

The mid-life crisis is like a coin with two sides, a bright and a dark side. I will start with the dark side, as that helps us to understand what is happening. But then I will come back to the vastly more important bright side.

WHEN AND HOW DOES THE 'SECOND CALL' APPEAR?

The 'second call' is like a new birth, after the time of youth.

The time of youth
Youth is the time when the great choices are made: type of work, marriage, religious consecration, commitment to work for the

church or a community. These choices are sustained by the ease of the gift, by inexperience of limitation, by the extent to which one can be influenced by the example of those around and ahead of us. There is a correspondence between the generosity proper to a youthful temperament and the call of Jesus to leave all and follow him. People receive great graces, they go out to preach, they found movements or institutions, or they find the rock on which to build their life.

The weaknesses of youth can be of several kinds. There is, of course, inexperience, but also the difficulty of respecting what there is of good in being subject to authority. What happens is that young people rely a great deal on themselves. Their sensibility can predominate their make-up. The body, even if it is prepared to make the sacrifice, also has its claims. Impatience for tangible results can make us drive on through the ups and downs that occur. Insecurity, affective or material, while it can be a driving force, can also hold one back.

Fr Voillaume, who had great experience of the spiritual life in general and of community life in particular, has some apt comments on this period: 'In the first stage we have not yet experienced the human and natural *impossibility* in our situation of living according to the supernatural order of the [evangelical] counsels.[5] During youth, there is a correspondence between the generosity natural to that age and the call of Jesus to leave everything to follow him [...]. As well as which, the divine pedagogic skill of the master who calls us will help to sustain us in a provisional illusion[6] without which perhaps no one would have the courage to leave everything to follow Jesus and carry his cross.'

In other words, the young person thinks that everything is possible; he or she goes forward with courage but, unconsciously, remains very much attached to the self. Young people may not take the exact measure of their weaknesses and their sin. But, the mystic Tauler observes, 'People can do as they please, and try as they will, but they do not attain real peace, they cannot become people of heaven in a real sense, before they are forty. Before that, they are worn down by all sorts of things, and their natural inclinations get in the way on this side and on that; and what happens in oneself is often due to oneself alone, although people imagine it is entirely from God; before that age, it is not possible truly and fully to attain peace, nor to be completely heaven-centred.'[7] In other words, even in the case of the holiest and most obedient of people, it takes time to build things up and to get rid of the depths of egoism and pride that drag us down. People can consider themselves radical, and want to be so, but they remain only half-committed. And then one day the hidden reality traps us again.

This is not to say that during the first part of life's journey there will not be any trials. There are, for several reasons: first, the fact of trying to form oneself implies an effort that can fail; and then, there are wounds in our personality that are not completely healed; and finally, there are spiritual trials, like the 'nights' that often occur during this period. But we overcome all these with time and the grace of God. We can then have the sense of ourselves as 'well' people, so to speak. But that is only part of the truth. There is still work to be done. For one thing, one never knows oneself completely, and for another, when people do discover their weaknesses, they are often very harsh with themselves.

Not that any of this should lead people to think that youth is merely a time of illusion, even spiritual illusion, or that one is necessarily wrong. No, youth is the time of giving, and that is important.

The time of challenge
When one becomes older, a new attitude appears, that of wisdom, which allows a better view to be taken of things. But the first thing we see, rightly, is how much sin and limitation still remains in us. This comes about in a rather curious way.

For the 'second call', time is needed. In general, for those who live in community, it takes a number of years of community living and minimum age. Let us say that it would be very exceptional in people of less than thirty-five years of age and ten or fifteen

THE 'SECOND CALL'

years of community life. But it can come to people of twenty years or more of community life. God has his time! In any case, it is not to be made into an absolute necessity or an obligation. There can be a fruitful and happy community life without experiencing a 'second call'.

With time and the grace of the Lord, says Father Voillaume, imperceptibly everything begins to change. Human enthusiasm gives way to a sort of unconcern regarding supernatural realities; the Lord seems more and more distant from us and some days we find boredom taking over; we are tempted more easily to pray less, or to do so routinely. Chastity causes us difficulties we had not envisaged; there are some new temptations; we feel a certain heaviness and more easily go in search of sensual satisfaction. Moreover, we will have a tendency, instinctively and not even noticing it, not to see any harm in that, and to live a rather more independent life, without taking much account of our superiors. Being open [with them] seems less necessary, and charity more difficult.[8]

Let us consider some manifestations of this crisis. We notice a kind of lassitude, of disgust, at least a heaviness, less facility in meeting our obligations, a lessening of enthusiasm, sometimes bitterness. This is linked to a turning in on oneself, related to personal problems, or those of the couple, or the family, and to the feeling that what one has done up to this has not been so useful. To take a few remarks at random:

'No one takes any notice of what I do.'
'I have not really been converted.'
'I have used up all that my family (my work, my community, my commitment to the church ...) could give me.'
'If others knew what I was really like.'
'What is going to become of me?'
'I am no good for anything anymore.'
'I am not recognised, no one takes notice of what I have to give.'
'The parish (my movement, my community ...) is not well run.'

'Did I make the wrong choices?'
'My family (my work-place, my community ...) is harming me,'
'I have discovered my brothers' faults, and things are not good.'
'I have been dropped.'
'Basically my commitment was based more on attraction than on personal choice.'
'I'm not going forward, I'm going back.'
'It is time to prepare my retirement.' And so on ...

Such remarks could be multiplied. As Tauler wrote: 'All the holy thoughts and pleasant images and the joy and jubilation and all that God may have given a person, it all begins to seem displeasing, and he feels himself excluded from everything, to the point that he gets no satisfaction out of anything and has no desire to stay there; what he has, he does not want, and what he wants, he does not have, and he is trapped between two extremes in great pain and torment.'[9] However, there is no need to apply it all to oneself too quickly. When medical students first learn about tropical diseases they imagine they have all the symtoms themselves, without ever being near the tropics! But something in the list given may strike a chord. Sooner or later it will. Criticism, disgust, pessimism, make themselves felt, even in people who thought themselves well past that stage. Christ's words about the salt losing its savour seem to apply ... So?

HOW TO REACT? FIRST, INAPPROPRIATE REACTIONS

There will naturally be a reaction when a person reaches this situation. But usually it will not be appropriate, because one is out of sorts. And, especially, because there is no personal fault in the matter. People did what they thought they should do. 'The most upsetting thing, 'days Fr Voillaume, 'is that the more we have been generous and faithful to grace, the more blocked our way forward seems to be.' In other words, our spiritual past has been so good that it is not adapted to helping us in our present state. So we may react in such ways as the following.

The temptation to compromise

Fr Voillaume expresses this well:

> The risk of the passage of time is that there is a certain wear and tear on ideals and on the expenditure of effort to realise them, for us as in any undertaking, and this will lead us to settle for mediocrity in the matter of holiness. Time and maturity of years bring with them the temptation to compromise between the supernatural demands of the Saviour's love and those of our adult human selves. Each year more of us reach this stage, the stage when we can make for the last time the choice between Jesus and the world, between heroic charity and mediocrity, between the cross and a certain comfort, between holiness and moderate fidelity to religious commitment. Indeed this is the stage the whole community is reaching.

This applies to every commitment, every movement or community: the work can still get done, but the meaning gets lost. In a way, of course, it is easier to go on, and to survive: but let there be no more talk of anything radical!

Flight

Flight is another way of reacting, almost a classical way. Even in the Middle Ages it was noted as a great temptation at this stage of the spiritual life. The problem can no longer be faced. So, run away from it. This can be done in several ways, such as the following.

Flight forward: 'Because he [the religious] does not want to reform himself, he wants to reform the community,' says Tauler. 'He projects outside himself the discontent that he feels regarding himself and he obstructs by exterior reforms his own access to the depth of his soul.'

Flight towards new forms of spiritual life: This is also quite a classical form of evasion. 'The outpouring of the Spirit is not enough for me, I need something more. The forms of community spirituality are not enough for me, I need others.' Fashionable phenomena can come into play in this matter, even within the community. The new is welcomed, but soon it is no longer enough.

Or, flight towards involvement, movement or simply towards community. However, the fact that this is a danger does not mean people should sit back and stop searching for the new manifestations of God's will. The important thing to remember is that whatever disrupts unity needs serious questions asked of it.

Obstructionism

Another way of reacting to the mid-life crisis consists in not budging, setting ones face against any new step on the road of development and relying entirely on the former way of life. On the psychological plane, this reaction leads to the taking of a stand on principles, and hiding behind them out of fear of change. On the religious plane, obstructionism appears as hardening of attachment to older exercises of piety.[10]

The flight into formalism can be expressed like this: 'I do not know what is happening to me, so I cling more tightly to my commitments, even if I do not understand them.' Indeed, it makes good sense not to change when one is not clear what to do, but there is no use in holding on to things frantically.

Other ways of reacting or ways of expressing those kinds of reaction could, no doubt, be found. Anger, for example, is certainly at times a form of flight. And of course they can be combined, together or successively

Certainly, not all the problems the ancient writers already knew have to do with the 'second call'. Discernment is needed, with the help of a spiritual director. But when the symptoms mentioned above appear, the question of a 'second call' should be considered.

HOW TO REACT IN A GOOD WAY?

What is God doing?

In all these cases, the thing to do is to remain calm and then go further. That is where God awaits us. What has already been achieved is only a preparation of the ground. As Fr Voillaume says so well:

> Above all, I would wish you to be convinced that the discouragement, the heaviness, of your spiritual life, which you feel tempted to or even subject to within, *is not a sign of the end of anything generous, but, on the contrary, the sign of a new call of the Lord. One stage has been passed, and this time it will be decisive.*[11]

It is indeed now that we are going truly and only to God:
> In truth I tell you, when you were young, you put on your own belt, and went where you would; when you are old, you will stretch our your hands, and someone else will put your belt on you and lead you where you would rather not go. (John 21:18)

But why does Jesus do that?

In the gospel of St John, one of the categories used by Christ to describe mankind's situation in face of God is the opposition 'from above/from below'. This is especially true in the great discourse to Nicodemus. Thus he declares: 'I tell you, anyone who is not born from above cannot see the Kingdom of God.' (Jn 3:3) 'Do not be astonished because I said you must be born from above.' (Jn 3:7) 'He who comes from above is above all; he who is of the earth is earthly and speaks in an earthly way. He who comes from heaven bears witness to what he has seen and heard, and no one accepts his witness.' (Jn 3:31f)

We do not take these oppositions seriously enough.[12] We like to count ourselves among the 'spiritual' people, those who know something about life 'from above'. But the opposition remains, and we are not in fact entirely 'from above'. Then gradually or suddenly a difficult situation arises, even a real crisis, of the kind described above.

The essence of the crisis is a great stripping away. We have worked hard for the Lord. Both the word 'conversion' and its reality are familiar to us. And now our ideal of sanctity seems impossible of attainment! We have nothing left. We have given so much, staked everything on God! We have left so much! God has promised us so much, even here on earth! It is true that we have seen with our eyes the wonders of God. But now, here we are, after all that, in an impasse. Where are the promises of God?

That is exactly the point. The promises of God are entering into a new phase of realisation, a much deeper one. *We are on the way from the level of having to the level of being, from the level of action so as to gain recognition to the level of life in the truth.* It is now that we are attaining a true understanding of the depth of our sin, and with it a sort of vertigo above the abyss. But it is also now that the Lord is taking us into his intimacy. *It is now that we are really discovering the mercy of God.* As the country priest of Bernanos says, 'All is grace.' And the greatest grace we can experience in life, greater than the grace of success, greater than the grace of virtue, is the grace of mercy, the grace of salvation.

This is precisely the moment when we are to accept, not our saving of ourselves, but our being saved, and that by pure grace. This experience is absolutely crucial in a journey towards sanctity. *It is nothing new.* We have always been told it, and we always knew it. But now we are experiencing it more radically. We are on the way to lay aside our cloak of misery ('Jerusalem, Jerusalem, leave aside your robe of sorrow!') and put on the white garments of salvation.

Basically what is happening to us is the very experience of the cross. In the first part of our life, the cross is present, but usually it is not central. Now it begins to bear our full weight. The experience of the cross has of course two aspects. First, it is a death, and a real death. It is not to some *thing* that we die, but to ourselves. And then, the cross is glorious. It gives life. How? Because on it we accept the mercy of God. In a way, by accepting this mercy, we make the cross produce its effect. Always remember that the great anguish that Jesus suffered at Gethsemane, as he confided to St Margaret Mary, was that his cross was of no avail, that his mercy was not accepted. And it is not accepted because fundamentally we think that we can rescue ourselves from sin by our own efforts. Then the moment arrives when it becomes clear that there is no avoiding mercy. There is no more room for illusion. The only thing to do is follow the example of

Thérèse Martin, and throw ourselves into the arms of the mercy that is there for us. Then, we rise to new life with God.

One day, Jesus said something like this to St Margaret Mary: 'You have not given me everything. – But, yes, Lord, I have given you everything! – No, you have not given me your sin.' Everything is found in that. When someone gives his sin, *he experiences a sort of 'second birth'*, as Tauler said. He enters a new life, the one the Saviour promised to Nicodemus. That is being really born 'from above'.

What should we do?
The first thing is *to look reality in the face*. And reality, for now, is our sin, that is, everything unconverted in us. That is what we are like. After so many years of effort, there is still all that conversion to go through. If we run away from it, we will make no further progress. There is no point is making a drama out of how things are, but it is important to have the courage to face it.

Carl Gustav Jung said that in the first part of life, someone builds himself or herself up in reference to a personal project, a self-image, an ideal to be incarnated and personalised. This ideal comes from education, from oneself, or elsewhere. That makes sense, and concerns what he calls the *persona*. This ideal is thus a mask, which is what 'persona' means. It is protection against the external world. But in fact everyone has a shadow side: that too makes good sense. 'This shadow is composed of psychic aspects of the human being that are in part inhibited, and in part not experienced or hardly experienced...'[13] The time comes in life when the shadow appears. If we accept it, then we become truly human people. We no longer live for the sake of recognition, but accept all the dimensions of our being, and thus become free.

The second thing is not to look at oneself, but at Jesus. That is at once the result of a decision, of effort, and, especially, of the gift of God. Knowing that one is full of sins, one now goes a step further: in a sense, one turns one's back on oneself.

The third thing is *to accept the cross* – not to wallow in suffering. The cross is glorious, it saves us. Accepting that we are sinners, but 'mercied' sinners. The cross is the place of salvation. No longer to live without referring ourselves to the cross, in an act of continual praise, of constant gratitude, all the stronger because we know how much we are risking.

Another dimension is often joined to the cross – *sacrifice*, following St Thérèse: offering our sufferings and our difficulties for the salvation of souls. For her, that gave the cross its real meaning. As the years go by, new crosses appear. If they are offered, they give our human and spiritual lives a quite new orientation.

The fourth thing is *to renew our desire*, and in particular our desire for sanctity. Desire, like everything else, is renewed. The Holy Spirit is given again. If we do not have any desires, let us ask for the 'desire to desire'. If there is no desire, nothing moves. The angel Gabriel called the prophet Daniel *vir desideriorum*, a man of desires. This is essential. God's response is pitched at the level of our desire. 'You provide the capacity, I will provide the flood', the Lord said to St Catherine of Siena. And for that purpose, seek a very simple kind of holiness, like St Thérèse.

In the fifth place, *make acts of faith*. Even if one feels in the deepest blackness, go forward in naked faith. Tell the Lord again that one has confidence in him, that he can act and that he will act. Thank him for it in advance. Refuse discouragement or sadness. Fight unceasingly against sentiments that are not inspired by God. Put up with having no perceptible graces to rely on.

In the sixth place, *accept the idea of death*. We are entering into the decisive phase of our life, that which prepares us for the great transition. We want to pass that gate as saints. For that precise reason, think of death. Not with fear, not with too much imagining. This thought can put everything in perspective and, far from immobilising us, give us more fervour.

> *Giving oneself in death*
> We are called to give ourselves not only in life, but also in death. And, as the well-beloved children of God, we are called to make of our death our greatest gift [...] As well-beloved sons and daughters of God, we discover that death

permits us to make the complete discovery of our identity as well-beloved. For those who know themselves to have been chosen, blessed and broken so as to be given, death is the outstanding way to become a true gift for others.[14]
Henri Nouwen (1932-1996)

What are the particular graces that God gives us during this period?
A grace of contemplation. This is perhaps the most important. Up to that we make acts of adoration, we have times of prayer. Now, if we remain faithful to our prayer commitments, we become really, in our being, in our permanent interior attitude, adorers, or, as Marthe Robin said of a priest, 'living prayers'. We are in a 'state' of adoration, as Jesus always was before his Father, like Pierre Gousat who 'was consumed in adoration', because he was permanently in this state. There is no need to be afraid to speak of the 'contemplative life' in relation to this period of existence, even if action remains. The 'Carmelites in the world' expression is sometimes used.

A grace of goodness, kindness, tolerance. When someone has nothing left to defend, and doesn't want any particular position, or recognition, at too high a cost, that person is free. God frees his or her heart and gives real goodness. It is good to see some old people whose expression and attitude only show goodness, understanding and welcome. The world of today, where there is much anguish and conflict, needs goodness. If older people do not diffuse it around themselves, no one will live. Goodness, kindness, is one of the most delicate manifestations of charity. This is the time to incarnate the first commandment in the second.

This new love for others will benefit us too. We become more vulnerable, defend ourselves much less, do not seek so much to make an impression but, in return, we will receive much more support from others.

A new grace of service. More detached, more free, more generous. It is like being renewed in humility. Even the most humble services no longer put us off. We go wherever we are needed, and not where we think we are needed. That brings plenty of surprises. Sometimes it is the start of a new life of service.

TWO TESTIMONIES

The testimony of Chloé

It was during my university studies that I met the religious community in which I was professed twenty years ago. That corresponded to a powerful encounter with the Lord, which led me to invest myself totally in this new family.

I moved along step by step, by means of fraternal life, which was a source of healing for me: I felt myself loved just as I was! Quickly enough, I attained a certain human and spiritual equilibrium, which allowed me to progress and to undertake certain responsibilities in the Congregation. Some years ago, I reached a point where I felt myself completely fulfilled, the Lord being everything for me.

That was when an encounter, about five years ago, brought to light a profound weakness in my affective life. I began to sink as it were into an abyss, and I experienced such an interior torment that I sometimes questioned my sanity. All the reactions that I thought I had mastered for twenty years were let loose: jealousy, pride, desire for recognition, playing for attention, caprice, sulks, not to mention doubts against the faith ... All that brought me back in practice to an adolescent crisis that I had never deeply experienced. Mercifully, the Lord gave me the grace of being surrounded at that time with brothers who accepted me, sustained me, helped me. I was able quickly to confront the deep cause of my woundedness (in relation to my mother) and to be helped by a prayer for healing.

The Lord permitted that just after this episode, I changed my place of residence and of work and found myself in a place where Mary is very present. There I found myself a particular object of her attention, and I am certain that is what re-educated me and reconstructed me interiorly.

Now, someone looking at me could think there has been some regression in my spiritual life (a small example: while for-

merly I only read spiritual books, now I prefer Agatha Christie!). But the light of the Lord has shown me that the painful episode I passed through has borne fruit:
- looking at the truth about myself. I know that I used to have many illusions about myself. Now, like Thérèse, I am not astonished to find new weaknesses in my life. At the same time, I am much more accepting of who I really am. It seems that this is the way of true humility;
- greater openness to others, linked to a more peaceful attitude to myself, greater ease in forgetting self and being generous with myself;
- more tolerance for others, to whom I am inclined to be merciful as people were merciful with me;
- a faith (and a charity) more stripped of sensible support; the determination to go to the end with what I profess, even if that seems foolishness;
- and greater realism, also.

All that comes, I believe, from Mary's motherly education.

But I am confident that the Lord will bring to completion the work he has begun, since he has brought me through a decisive period, even after twenty years in community! It is he who will do everything: 'He is faithful, who calls you. It is still he who will do that.' (1 Thess 5:24)

Stephane's testimony

I have been a member for twenty-seven years of the Emmanuel Community. I have held several responsible positions in it, and looking back, I think I can say that I have found there, after a long search, the place of my happiness. I have always been, and still am today, very content in it. It is my family, they are my people.

In other words, I am not exactly in the category of a 'crisis' of confidence in the community. Still, I am thinking of a 'second call' for myself. How has this come about?

In years gone by, I made great efforts to build myself up, and community life has been a great help. A time came when I had the impression, by God's grace, of knowing myself and of being in command of myself, of being competent and accepted in my activity, especially in the religious domain, in brief, a period of maturity. I felt good from every point of view.

It was then that I found vulnerability. First, my own vulnerability, as a result of a series of events and discoveries about myself. I have been very much protected by God, and have not committed grave faults. But I also understood and saw clearly that I could easily have done so. For me that was a troubling and important discovery. At certain times, I was not quite sure who I was. I then discovered that I could not save myself by my own strength, but that I needed to be saved. And it was only by grace that I was saved. I had always known and even taught that, but it was another thing to know it in my own skin! I am sitting, like St Thérèse, at the table of sinners, and that is where I still am.

Another thing I discovered was the vulnerability of my brothers. I have realised that even solid and balanced people have their secret weaknesses that can some day become active. Nobody is made of steel.

I have certainly gained much greater humility and realism from these discoveries. I have been able to progress and to integrate them, thanks to the tactful love and the confidence of my brothers and sisters in community. And then the Lord asked me to go further, and tell him that I was ready to give my life for my brothers, if he asked me to. He has asked me to carry at least a part of the cross, for the love of him and of my brothers. I understood better that I was responsible, in part, for the holiness of the community. I could not recoil from the interior commitment that this implied. This has given me much greater motivation for the service I perform, and much greater confidence in the work of the Holy Spirit in the heart of the community.

At the moment I am called to make a greater offering of my pains, my sufferings and my joys. I am beginning to understand better that prayer is my most important activity. I am rediscovering the essential importance of praise and adoration. I understand that everything follows from my interior life, from a more profound intimacy with God whose invitation is, 'Come to me.' I am receiving also a new intimacy with Mary. And then, while I have always loved my brothers and sisters, I am receiving with age an affection for them that is gentler and more open. Yes, 'goodness' [kindness] seems to me the right word for what God is asking of me and giving me to live.

I am astonished at that. I was afraid that I would get withered with age, but what has happened is just the opposite. Thank you, Lord!

*

To know God is to love him and to approach him with one's heart, but, much more, it is to let oneself be approached by him. He is approaching us in fact. We are saved by pure grace, without any merit of ours being the initial cause of it. Now, we are convinced of that. Now the Lord, in the name of his mercy, wants us to go deeper and further.

The 'second call' means generous self-giving but it also means the taking note of what we are giving ourselves for, or rather for whom and to whom: for the Lord, for his church.

The 'second call' means agreeing to become transparent, handing ourselves over to others, sharing more simply what we live by, in a greater interior and exterior freedom.

The 'second call' is a call to greater charity. Our world no longer knows Christ. We are called to testify to him by the charity with which we live. We can only receive that charity from Jesus himself by basing our lives more fully on him in adoration and in listening to his Word.

So, let us not extinguish this new call of the Spirit in ourselves, which is just as important as the one we heard when we experienced for the first time the outpouring of the Spirit. Jesus must take up more and more space in us. Our whole life must be reorganised around him. He must become the centre. Let us allow the Holy Spirit to come himself and take possession of our heart, to get rid of whatever is not doing well there, to take away all that we want to hold on to, to put his own thoughts and his own action into a heart that no longer has anything of its own.

Let us accept being stripped, but also being filled with a new life which we do not know, and where God is more in control: 'Brothers, you are the house that God has built'. (1 Cor 3:9-17)

To conclude, remember that everything goes more surely and more speedily with the Virgin Mary. Let us re-consecrate ourselves to 'our mother in heaven'. Let us put our heart beside the Immaculate Heart of Mary. That is our place, and all will there be better, gentler and stronger.

> Lord Jesus Christ, Son of the living God, by the will of the Father and the power of the Holy Spirit, your death gave life to the world.
> May your Body and Blood deliver me from my sins and from every evil.
> May I remain faithful to your commandments and never be separated from you.

Prayer of the priest at Mass, before communion

CHAPTER NINE

Woundedness and spiritual life

Being wounded is part of being human. We are neither so smooth nor so tough that something will not break through our defences in the course of life. Most of these injuries (even quite serious traumas) we get over, but some of them leave an enduring mark on us. They can determine or at least affect our choices and our attitudes. If we have suppressed them, they can eventually resurface. All of which inevitably has consequences for our relationship with God.

In the present chapter, I do not want to provide a complete account of woundedness but only to point out certain connections between it and the spiritual life, so that we can have a better idea of how we stand in this regard.[1]

HOW ARE PEOPLE WOUNDED?[2]

The first thing to enquire is, who can wound us? This might seem an unnecessary question, but experience proves otherwise. Every day one can meet people who are visibly wounded but who do not know it, or prefer to deny it. So it is useful to shed some light on the matter. Here, I am only going to give some examples, simply to show people who are not familiar with the situation what can happen. The picture that emerges may seem bleak, but it should be remembered that for each cause of psychic injury, there is an opposite attitude that builds up and gives life. These positive attitudes are many, and are something to thank God for more than we usually do, perhaps because they are very ordinary in themselves.

As a rule, woundedness linked to childhood, especially early childhood, is the most harmful. It can reappear decades later.

This is not surprising, because the child has few if any defences. Children are like clay that can be moulded, and whatever happens to them can leave them with a lasting mark.

In the first place, things that date from before birth can harm people. This is the case when there are long-standing problems in a family that the children will eventually inherit: painful family secrets, lasting quarrels, involvement with evil spirits arising from superstitious practices, sexual ambiguities going back in time, recurrent anxieties, and so on. Such things can create a climate that the new-born child of course cannot analyse, but can notice.

We can be wounded by the circumstances of our conception: a child may be unwanted, or there may have been strange sexual practices. The child in the womb is dependent on the mother's emotional life and receives something from it. The mother's anguish can affect it, especially if it is linked to a possible abortion. Also, an unborn child can be aware of the mother's poor state of health to some extent. Finally, I believe that earlier abortions are not without their consequences.

The very act of birth is extremely important. A child must be welcomed, cared for. There can be medical problems relating to birth that eventually may prove traumatising, or the absence of the father, or coarseness and insensitivity on the part of the medical staff. Being born is in itself a shock for the new-born child, because it means leaving the gentle and protective environment of the womb for the world outside. The shock can be reduced or aggravated.

The welcome given to the child means that it does not feel abandoned, not only in its first days, but even in its first years. It must also feel that it is in a good place. If it is not well received by its siblings, or its mother does not care for it, or is separated from it by illness for a long time, there could be serious harm to the child.

The infant must experience love. People must smile at it, talk happily to it, touch it respectfully and kindly. In the absence of such contacts, it can have the sense of causing trouble, of not being loveable. And all that can become part of itself, so that later on it feels guilty of something, perhaps even guilty for existing. The child also experiences that there are rules and limits not to be broken: that there are sanctions. If this is not carefully managed, or if on the contrary it is entirely absent, there can be consequences later on. Children who are kings can later become adults who are unsociable and irresponsible.

The respective roles of the father and the mother are very important. The mother is the one who constructs the interior world; the father establishes clear points of reference and opens up the exterior world. An absent or unloving father is often a catastrophe whose repercussions are felt very late in life. A father who is present and plays his part builds up the child and gives it confidence in him.

> *The testimony of Jean Vanier*
> I had an experience when I was thirteen years old, a very powerful one that was like a new birth, my third birth. The first was when I was born, the second when I was baptised, and the third was when I wanted to enter the British Royal Navy.
>
> It was during the war, and we lived in Canada, so that it was necessary for me to cross the Atlantic at a time when one ship in three was sunk by German submarines. I went to my father and told him what I wanted to do. He asked me why. I do not know what I replied, but I have never forgotten what he said: 'I have confidence in you. If that is what you want, you must do it.'
>
> That day, he caused me to be born again. If he had confidence in me, then I too could have confidence in myself. If he had told me to wait until I was older, I would have waited, but I would have implicitly understood that my intuition was not reliable, that I could not trust myself. But he told me, 'I have confidence in you' and that helped me to trust myself and taught me to trust others.'

When a child goes to school, it is entering another world. There is the discovery of living with comrades who are sometimes hard or common. There is the need to defend oneself, to protect oneself, to wear a kind of social mask. Competition and evaluation make their appearance. There can be a good deal of academic pressure, and the need to succeed can take firm hold of the mind. A child needs to be encouraged and recognised for what it does well, and to have a positive view of itself so that it can get the best out of itself. This does not always happen. A child is extremely sensitive to injustices, falsehoods and hypocrisy.

Adolescents are idealists and see the world in a way that is perhaps schematic, but they have the desire to live for something worth the trouble. If they see this ideal mocked and at times betrayed by adults, they can suffer great disillusionment.

With the awakening of their affectivity, the adolescent or the young person encounters further ways of suffering injury. They may have a bad experience of sexuality, which is often the case nowadays because of society's preoccupations in this area. The world of sexuality is often very wounded, and at an ever younger age. Love affairs can work out more or less well, and bring their own failures and frustrations. A multiplicity of partners can at times give rise to feelings of betrayal or lead to the cultivation of indifference regarding others.

Adolescents need to be accompanied in an understanding way by the family. This is not always the case. Parents who are married can sometimes do harm to their children rather than sustain them or build them up. Not to mention what can happen where the parents are not married and their relation is less stable and so somewhat less reassuring. A divorce or a separation can be traumatic. And as well as all of this, children can also wound their parents: false pregnancies, premature deaths, children who cause disappointment, who turn out badly, who are often sick, who marry or have relations with partners who are unacceptable, and so on. And finally, there are those who would like to marry but cannot, which can give rise to suffering and frustration.

The area of finding one's place in the world, of seeking employment, of work, of success and failure, is evidently very significant in anyone's life. It can cause anguish, disappointment, and the destruction or alteration of one's sense of oneself.

More generally, social life can involve disappointment and injury stemming from the groups people belong to: societies, trade unions, and even one's country or an international organisation.

Existence itself entails grieving. Some partings are experienced well. Others are unbearable and can affect the whole of life. They can even be traumatic. For example I have known couples whose life revolved around the memory of an only child who died. There was nothing only that.

Then there are injuries to the intelligence. This is something little spoken of, but it is very real. Intelligence is designed to perceive the truth. It can be led astray by bad education, badly thought-out instructions, or a debased culture, to the point of mental blindness. Whole segments of the universe are then closed off to it. When someone tries to remedy that by adopting without thought whatever ideas are in fashion there can be a deep sense of reality eluding one and of being alone with one's illusions.

The area of life that is concerned with God is not immune to causing people wounds. One can find in priests or Christians or the church as a whole a source of disillusionment. One can feel betrayed or unrecognised. It is a delicate matter. Sometimes it can be or seem to be God who is the source of woundedness. He seems to have abandoned us. Or else not to have to created us as we would have liked to be, or in the place we would have wished.

Lastly, I can wound myself. First, my sins are a constant source of wounds, especially serious or repeated sins. Or, I would prefer to be someone else instead of who I am. Or, I have a certain image of myself, and one day it vanishes or explodes. This can be one of the greatest wounds a person could suffer. And of course there will be illnesses which in addition to being medical problems can cause psychological harm of different kinds.

HOW TO REACT TO THESE WOUNDS?

Good reactions

I hope it will not be too shocking to say that often people's reaction to such things as have been described above is good. There is an inner dynamic of the human person, the desire to live. It can me more or less strong depending on the individual and the society. In what are called third-world countries people manage very well in situations we could not endure: they have a tremendous hold on life.

Generally speaking, wounds are completely negative. They do harm, but we can transcend this harm. The wounds can drive us to progress, to build ourselves up, even if it is only because we do not want to continue feeling the pain.

In reality, the great means of healing most wounds is to come through them. The ability to do this is sometimes called 'resilience'. For example, if a child has difficulties at school, it will be good for him to concentrate on the areas where he feels more competent. If he succeeds in certain subjects, that may have an effect, in due course, on his weaker subjects. If I am made to feel foolish because I am bad at swimming, for example, I will do better than others in long distant running, perhaps. In the case of most wounds, we surmount the obstacle and make progress.

One of the advantages of this unconscious mechanism of healing wounds is that we do not have to be always thinking about our deficiencies. A moderately successful life can take us out of ourselves and brighten our outlook. It makes us available for other things besides our personal issues.

Bad reactions

Unfortunately, there are some wounds that people do not want to surmount or cannot. They harden into psychic cysts. Instead of surmounting or transcending them, one can be easily tempted to act out of them.

For example, a fifty-year-old man discovers one day that he has in himself an attitude of dependence. He defers to any authority he senses as paternal. There is something unfinished in his make-up. On reflection, he sees that his own father himself had a weak and incomplete side. Then he discovers that his paternal grandfather divorced and abandoned his wife and children. His father suffered from what was at that time a great shame and from his father's absence. It was all so traumatic that it was kept completely secret up to that point. The father was not able to construct himself properly and had then passed on this deficiency. In this case, the wound was transferred through several generations and could only be attended to when its causes finally became clear.

Again, a man was beaten by his father. The family was a violent one, even in speech they went to the limits of violence. The man had imbibed this attitude, and caused terror at school and at college. Later his whole life was marked by violence even in the way he spoke and carried out his work. He was able to wear the mask forced on him by social conventions, but in reality violence continued within him. He could not accept the love of others and would say that he was incapable of giving love.

Or again, a man succeeds in life, but he sometimes has a recurring dream: that of being in an absurd and difficult situation, and finding no way out. The dream ends in a kind of anguish. This gives him a permanent feeling that he can fail. One day, he sees that it is linked to his parents. It turns out that when he was born his mother was relatively old and his father an invalid. They thought they would never have a child. These words, 'We will never have one', hardened into an element of his deep psychology. The day when this comes to light and he can present it to God, he feels real liberation and from then on hardly ever has the dream again.

Wounds like these can be suppressed,or else entertained in a contaminating way. They may be merely personal, though I am convinced that there are also collective wounds, for example in families or in communities. I would go so far as to say that there are wounds that affect social groupings and even whole countries.

They can enter deeply into the unconscious and continually influence activity from there. The whole of psychoanalysis is based on this discovery. Thus they can influence attitudes in bonding with others, in shame, in dominance. Many abnormal human actions are, in my view, due to wounds that have never been identified and treated as such.

The wound of sin

Whilst it is true that any wounds a person suffers from will block or at least impede their life, still their freedom remains intact. There is always the possibility to do good, at least to some extent. A person can escape from his or her woundedness gradually by making free and positive choices. If, on the contrary, he or she continues in sin, that is, in negative choices, the woundedness grows worse. But only God knows what is in people's hearts and can discern what degree of fault there is in anybody's life.

Moreover, evil spirits make use of people's wounds, especially by means of the imagination. They infect the wounds, they make them almost permanent, and thus establish a strong hold over them. In spiritual reflection on wounds, one often comes across spirits of doubt, of violence, of sensuality, of pride, of blindness, and so on. I do not wish to enter here into the matter of praying for deliverance, but I know that it is sometimes needed to support or open the way to the healing of a wound.

None of these wounds help the spiritual life. They constitute a handicap that prevents us raising ourselves towards God, opening ourselves to others, and accepting ourselves. They close us in on ourselves, and make us hard. How could anyone have the heart of a child, a confident heart, if they were always turned in on themselves? How can someone trust if they always suspect themselves of being traitors?

Healed wounds[3]

Over the past several years, some practices for healing have been gradually put in place. They are of several types, and of course they are not in conflict with the psychotherapies nor do they always replace them.

To begin with, I would wish to state that many wounds are

spontaneously healed by a steady Christian life and especially a well-established life in community. When people decide to follow Jesus, they become involved in the reconstitution of their interior world. They find themselves or rediscover themselves in a coherent universe, with clear points of reference, where assistance is available. In particular, they find a universe where the principal rule of life is love. Now the human being is a well of love, or I should say a 'pump' of love. If someone's emotional reservoir is empty, as Ross Campbell says, things go badly with him and his wounds are incurable.[4] If a person feels loved and loves, if love becomes the law of his life, many wounds heal themselves. That is often seen in the case of people who become converted. It is very striking to see how hearts open, how pieces of armour fall off one by one, and how love gradually penetrates the person.[5]

An important element in the journey towards healing is forgiveness.[6] Forgiveness is a particular feature of Christianity and is a factor in healing, inasmuch as bitterness and the spirit of vengeance sustain the evil instead of curing it. It is then necessary to forgive others and – what is more difficult – to forgive oneself. Then it is necessary to recognise the wound and name it, to speak openly to someone about it, in this way establishing contact or 'complicity' with the wound. Then, while using psychological methods if they are needed, one must entrust oneself to God and draw on his grace and mercy. The Lord gives a new sense of things in this way. It can give one a new orientation in life, deeper and stronger, even in the wake of serious setbacks, or of cruel bereavements. A new life can begin, with God, with others, and with oneself.

In the spiritual journey, the healing of wounds takes place at all stages, even though there are privileged times. One of these can be at the beginning, when one sees one's life in a new light, and the most obvious of the wounds appears. But sometimes, at the end of some years of Christian life, at the time of joining a community or a monastery, or when one founds a family, wounds may reappear, to one's great surprise. Still, the fact that they make themselves felt in this way means that one has become free enough and feels in a secure enough place to allow them to appear. They can then be dealt with.

It can happen that the wounds combine with the 'nights'. God uses the sufferings they cause for the good of our soul. But it is not to be too readily thought that every emergence of a wound is a mystical trial. In this matter, it is necessary always to remain modest and prudent.

Unhealed wounds and spiritual life
The magnificent text of St Paul in which he speaks of a wound that was not healed despite his begging God for healing is well known. There is nothing negative about his testimony, because he finds in this situation an opportunity for humility. Equally it permits him to experience the strength of God. The wound does not prevent him pursuing his mission, nor does it paralyse his spiritual life. On the contrary, precisely because of this humility, the wound actually helps him to progress. It is striking, when reading St Paul's text, to see how much the non-healing of the wound is linked to his spiritual life, and connected to the very high degree of life with God to which the Lord has introduced him.

> *St Paul's Testimony*
> To keep me from being too elated, a thorn was given to me in the flesh, a messenger of Satan to torment me, to keep me from being too elated. Three times I appealed to the Lord about this, that it would leave me, but he said to me, 'My grace is sufficient for you, for power is made perfect in weakness.' So I will boast all the more gladly of my weaknesses, so that the power of Christ may dwell in me. Therefore I am content with weaknesses, insults, hardships, persecutions, and calamities for the sake of Christ: for whenever I am weak, then I am strong.
> (2 Cor 12:7-10)

This signifies that there are wounds that we shall keep in spite of every treatment. Nonetheless, the Lord gives the strength to bear them and to transcend them. They are there, they trouble us, but they do not prevent us from living. They destroy neither our mission nor our life with God. The example of Marthe Robin is one among many others to bear witness to that.

On the other hand, in a spiritual journey, at a certain moment – often during the 'night of the spirit', it seems to me – we discover our deeper woundedness, what remains in us of radical poverty, of weakness that we thought we had surmounted. Our weakest point is not always the one we would have expected. We are then confronted with a radical choice. Either we deny it, and embark on flight and illusion, which could lead to the blocking or even a regression of our whole spiritual life, and its decline; or we agree to look steadily at this weakness under the eyes of God. It cannot have been easy for St Peter, with all his impetuosity and bravado, to see how much cowardice there still remained in him. What we then do is welcome 'the poor person hidden in ourselves', and enter into the complete truth about ourselves, in our own deepest self. Maybe we had thought that as we grew in the spiritual life, we would discover new treasures in the depth of ourselves, instead of which what we discover is an immense poverty. But we place it, in total powerlessness, under the merciful eye of Jesus, if we believe that he really, truly and by nature is the Saviour. Then we no longer avert our eyes from the face of Jesus, and we find we can accept ourselves, because God is sustaining us and enabling us to advance further.

> *An inverted ladder*
> The ladder of holiness is inverted, it leads downwards, it always descends further into the abyss of nothing and of littleness. We had perhaps imagined perfection as a matter of progression and climbing, but climbing like this, the effect of our own will, is exactly the opposite of Christian holiness, because it could so easily become our climb. We could falsely believe that our generosity and our good will are capable of making saints of us, and forget the 'without me you can do nothing' of Jesus.
> *André Daigneault*

Wounds 'turned round'

Ultimately it comes about that God 'utilises' wounds to facilitate a person's mission. He turns the wounds around, in a sense. From the difficulties they originally were, they become occasions of progress in the interior life and in one's mission.

To explain what I mean, I would like to take the example of St John Bosco (1815-1888). John Bosco was an exceedingly gifted child, charming, intelligent, amusing, physically strong and agile. But he belonged to a poor family and his father died when he was very young. This left him in an very difficult situation: no work, no chance of study, no prospects. He was in the same situation as thousands of rural children at the beginning of the nineteenth century, who had nowhere to turn except to remain uneducated and take manual work, whether by becoming domestic servants in the country, or migrating to the unfamiliar life of the towns and becoming industrial workers in wretched conditions. John Bosco was thus a wounded child: no father, family disagreement regarding him, no future, no social standing, no priests to help him or at least, not many, because of their reserved and distant manner. He was a child ignored.

But he had faith, and he had unbelievable vitality and the desire for life. The Holy Spirit already lived in him. He succeeded in getting an education and decided to aim for the priesthood. He founded the Congregation of the Salesians (in honour of St Francis de Sales, as we have seen) and that of the Daughters of Mary Auxiliatrix (Salesian Sisters of St John Bosco) for the education of children in trouble. The most violent opposition and the worst obstacles never stopped him: he turned them all round or reversed them. He became one of the most effective and prolific saints of modern times. With his followers, he educated tens of thousands of young people and contributed in an unequalled way to the balance and progress of society. He became a benefactor of souls and of humanity.

In the soul and the psychology of John Bosco, God had 'turned round' his wound. John knew all too well what it was not to have a father, or anyone who could take his part in an effective way. He knew what exclusion and being a non-person meant. He was himself a father for young people, and gave them what a father gives: confidence, instruction, an opening to the future, an ideal to strive for; he lived as an example for them and showed them the road of faith. There are wounds that have a part to play in the plan of God and which a person can make good use of on the way to holiness.

CHAPTER TEN

Extraordinary events in the spiritual life

Fr De Lubac once wrote: 'Mystical experience is not a luxury. Without it, the moral life runs the risk of being sheer inhibition, asceticism mere dryness, docility a half-conscious existence, and religious practice just routine.' He put it strongly, but he had reason to. By 'mystical experience' he meant whatever leads to contemplation, to the soul's union with its God, and such experience is normal. But the term 'mystical' also has another meaning. It stands for extraordinary events that occur in the spiritual life, not only 'sometimes' but to my mind, 'relatively often'.[1] Something must be said about them.

WHY DEAL WITH THEM?

A reality that cannot be concealed

There is a natural reluctance to speak of extraordinary events in the spiritual life for fear of being thought an *illuminé*, a hyper-charismatic. Nonetheless, it must be recognised that such things occur. 'Facts are stubborn things' as the historian's adage puts it. They upset things. It is enough to have a little familiarity with contemplative communities or even the Charismatic Renewal to come across this kind of fact. Spiritual discernment therefore supposes some degree of openness to them.

It is quite clear, however, that the core and substance of the spiritual life does not consist in manifestations of this order. It is right to insist and repeat constantly that no one should pray for them. But that does not allow us to despise them or to act as if they did not exist, because God does what he pleases and knows better than we why he sends them to people. So it would be a mistake to disregard them. Again, it is possible to become confused about them. Ignoring this kind of divine communication leaves a believer feeling uneasy. What is worse, things to do with psychic disorder or the paranormal will be mistaken for spiritual events. St John of the Cross said that the majority of these phenomena were false. I quite believe it.[2] But how could that be decided in the absence of any reflection and knowledge on the point? It is easy to pass from scepticism to naïvety. Unhealthy curiosity is extremely dangerous and peripheral to true spirituality, but incompetence is an equal danger to souls. As Cardinal Journet said, 'All the mystics are dangerous to read, but the risk is worth running.'

Whether one likes it or not, reflection on the subject can hardly be avoided. This is all the more so because of the whole tradition of competence and good sense that exists in the church, and that continues in current theology and studies of mystical phenomenology.[3]

Why do they happen?

We can begin by asking why God uses this way of dealing with us. A first response is that human nature, being very limited, is baffled and overcome by various other kinds of phenomenon in any case, as is certainly true. It is probably in such phenomena that the contact between the normal, the paranormal and the grace of God occurs, and it is an area requiring a great deal of discernment. But that is not quite enough, because God is all-powerful and could manifest himself perfectly in the depths of the soul without using such means.

Another response, which I think is correct, is that God is free and wishes to manifest himself without ceasing. We would like God to fit into our collective mental categories. Because we fear the supernatural, which might make us look ridiculous, we ask him to handle us carefully that area. He is under no obligation to do so. This is why he sometimes performs miracles that people of good faith, or even unbelievers, can accept without any prejudice.[4] In the spiritual life, which is completely under his guidance, God sometimes needs to affirm this supreme liberty that we would prefer him not to manifest. Spiritual phenomena break boundaries and open the way to God.

Extraordinary manifestations have also the advantage of saving time. Thanks to them, the Lord goes straight to the point. He 'attacks' at once several of the zones of being, even them all, and delivers a strong and comprehensible message to the person concerned. Such manifestations overcome a person's resistance so that he or she will progress more quickly. For example, the stigmata configures someone to Jesus, body and soul, with a quite particular intensity. Interior words and images, especially of a certain strength, manifest the presence of God in an extremely powerful way.

Finally, there are some extraordinary manifestations that are linked to a special vocation. This is the case with prophecy or knowledge or, less often, visions that can be seen by the external senses, as were those of Bernadette at Lourdes or those of the children of Fatima. In general, it is necessary always to distinguish manifestations linked to personal growth, which relate especially to the gifts of the Holy Spirit, from those given with a view to the good of the church, which relate more to the charisms.

Different kinds of extraordinary phenomena
What we have just said assumes that there are different categories of extraordinary phenomena. We are here in the presence of a vast and complex subject, which I will not try to simplify. Nonetheless there are at least two kinds to take note of.

The first is that of really very extraordinary phenomena which are only rarely encountered. Examples are the stigmata, levitation (being raised above the earth), phenomena of smell, of not eating for long periods, phenomena of light, miraculous communions, multiplication of hosts or of bread, the transporting of things or people, bilocation,[5] and so on. These constitute the class of the extraordinary among the extraordinary. In this book I will not deal with them, as our concern is with what affects the ordinary spiritual life: there are good recent books on the subject.[6]

On the other hand, there are more ordinary phenomena that are still extraordinary, if I may so express it. It is of these that I would like to speak here, for reasons of practice and discernment. It is good to know that these phenomena can intersect. In addition, it is rare for them to be 'chemically pure'. They affect the 'deep self', but they also affect all the other zones of the human person, which it is necessary frequently to remember.

The criteria for discernment
The usual criteria for discernment accepted in the church apply to these phenomena too, and we simply mention them here:
- The conformity of the phenomenon with the faith of the church regarding doctrine and morals;
- The trustworthiness of the person: his human and religious genuineness, his surroundings, his steadiness of mind, and his not standing to gain anything from the experience;
- The lasting peace and serenity that surround the person concerned in the phenomena;
- The person's capacity to obey both his spiritual director and the leadership of the church in general, within the limits of appropriate freedom and responsibility;
- The positive results that ensue from it: growth of virtues and gifts, in particular the increase of humility, fraternal love and the love of God.

THE PHENOMENA OF THE PRESENCE OF GOD

The most usual form
In my view, the most usual spiritual phenomenon is that of the presence of God perceived in the soul. I have already spoken of it above.

The phenomenon is simple. What happens most often is that a person 'senses' God's presence. Sometimes God is sensed as being at one's side: even if there is strictly no question of seeing anything, there is some location of the presence. More often it is within one, as at the centre of the soul. The presence makes itself felt. It is like having someone in the same room as you: the person is there, that is all. One could drive the presence away, by some means, but that would signify being somehow estranged from God.

It is certainly true that there can be illusions in this matter. For this reason it is necessary to seek assistance and verification. But the imagination does not produce at all the same effect as the real presence of God. An imaginative image is, so to say, exterior, peripheral, fluctuating, tense. It lacks objectivity and savour. In the presence of real divinity there is what we may call an anointing by God, gentle, clear, objective and peaceful, which can easily be recognised. God has his very typical way of being. It is quite clear that it is God and not someone else who is present.

When I say 'God', that means most often one or other of the Three Divine Persons. They are recognised and identified without difficulty. Each has his own manner of being and of making himself present. But sometimes also it is simply the Divinity who makes his presence strongly felt.

The presence of God can come and go. It can last for months and then depart. Its going is no small deprivation. Usually, one feels the lack of it so much that one asks God to return. One feels in some way outside of oneself. On the other hand, some people I know have experienced the grace of this presence, day and night, for years.

The presence of God can be accompanied by a more or less precise feeling, such as relations or friends feel for each other. For example, the love of God can be experienced as warm or as painful. One can feel expectation, desire, need, reproof. One can also feel the kindness, benevolence and mercy of God. When God shows his kindness like this, it is heart-melting.

The degree of God's presence is variable. Sometimes it is so strong that it can overwhelm one's life in seconds. That is what happens in conversions like that of St Paul, of Paul Claudel in Notre-Dame de Paris, and of Pierre Goursat. I have myself come across more than one example of this. Sometimes, being 'taken' by God in this way is almost unbearable. One person I knew was praying at St Peter's in Rome, and felt such a presence of Jesus that she thought she physically could not bear it, and prayed Jesus to stop it. Which he did. She was going through a difficult time, and this experience of his presence was very consoling for her. It remained as it were engraved on her soul for years.

The presence of God cannot be 'produced', but one can prepare for it and cultivate it. A seventeenth-century Carmelite brother in Paris, Laurence of the Resurrection, has shown how to dispose oneself for this presence and preserve it when it comes.[7] Clearly, if one makes light of it, it will vanish.

A stronger form

It sometimes happens that the presence of God makes itself more strongly felt, that it is more penetrating. The word that is used in such cases is 'ecstasy' or, if the experience is more violent, 'rapture'. To tell the truth, I do not like to use these words and I advise spiritual directors never to tell anyone that he or she has ecstasies.[8] In the present cultural context, to do so would not be helpful: it will be enough to see if that is the case and then gently to offer them assistance.

What happens in an ecstasy is that God makes himself present to such an extent, so closely and so pleasantly, that one does not wish to move. One quite simply remains with him. I do not like those pictures that show saints as if they were outside themselves, because it seems to me that what happens is generally much simpler than that. I knew a housewife who came to a prayer group and who, as soon as the meeting began, could no longer move. Jesus was present to her, and she remained with him. She would stand, sing, and sit, but all that was exterior. Interiorly Jesus was completely present to her. I also knew a businessman who, one day at home, remained for three-quarters of an hour on a step of his stairs. He was able to move but he did not want to. Jesus was within him, and he was content to be still with his eyes closed.

Except for certain particularly spiritual people, ecstasies do not last long nor come very often. But they mark the soul as it were with a seal. The soul's memory retains this valuable gift and dwells on it when necessary. However it is essential to verify these phenomena from the increase of the virtues in the heart of the person who receives them, and especially the growth of charity.

> *A Saint's reflection*
> When you see people who have such consolations in prayer that they rise outside and above themselves as far as God, and yet, have nothing ecstatic about the way they live, meaning by that a life raised and attached to God by the denial of their worldly desires and the mortification of their wishes and natural inclinations by interior gentleness, simplicity, humility and especially by continual charity, you can be sure that all these consolations are highly questionable and dangerous.
> St Francis de Sales (1567-1622)

Other phenomena of presence
There are other phenomena that have to do with presence: presence of the Virgin Mary, of the saints and of angels.

The Virgin Mary appears very rarely to people's physical eyes. Nevertheless, she very often manifests her presence. It is possible to 'meet' her, as it is to 'meet' Jesus, except that it is meeting a human being and not God. Such encounters can be very powerful and change the whole course of a life. Mary is present in a very clear way, as a person and not as an idea, with all her goodness, definiteness, vigour and consideration. Her presence goes and comes. Mary's friendship is so strong that if she moves away for a long period, it is very difficult to endure. We are not happy when our friends hide from us. On the other hand, when God gives someone the favour of the presence of Mary, it is a real happiness!

> *A testimony of Mary's presence*
> It was at a time when I had to make a decisive choice in my life. I believed that I had received a call from God in a particular direction, I had accepted it, I had discerned it with my

spiritual director, I had committed myself in this direction with all my energy, although it cost me a great deal. Thus, it seemed that my future was marked out. One day I made a pilgrimage to the Virgin at the sanctuary closest to my native town. I was praying quietly when I 'felt' the presence of Mary with an incredible suddenness and clarity. I did not see her, but the presence was very precise and localised: as if she came from the direction of the statue venerated in that place. But that was not the most surprising thing. This presence was accompanied by a requirement. The requirement did not take an intellectual form, but I could translate the intuition in the following question: 'And if what you have chosen does not come about, will you accept that?' I could not refuse Mary, who had meant so much in my life. I replied: 'Yes, I will accept it.' Nevertheless, no other way of living my life seemed possible. And yet, that is exactly what happened. In a completely unexpected way, my life took a different course. I had to accept a new direction that I had never thought of, and which took over from the former one. I have to say today, at a distance of years, that this new direction brought me happiness to a point that I could never have suspected, and I thank the Virgin for having prepared me for this new departure.

The presence of one saint or another in someone's life is equally common. These are friendships from heaven, sometimes ones we have not even looked for, and which establish themselves gradually. I would almost say that some saints are specialists in such friendship, like St Joseph or St Thérèse of the Child Jesus, or perhaps Marthe Robin. A saint is a friend, a guide, and intercessor. Each makes God present in their own way, and shows God's concern for us.

The presence of an angel at one's side is equally very precious in life if God grants it. Most often it is the guardian angel whose presence God reveals to the eyes of the soul. At times, he reveals even his name. Now, that is very useful, for the angels' names are the names of their missions. If we know their names, we also know the names of their missions in our regard. One of my friends was praying in a chapel in the United States when God revealed to him the name of his angel. He came out of the chapel when an American came up to him and said: 'When I was praying, just now, God told me the name of your angel.' It was the same! (That is called a confirmation.) I know people who enjoy the company of their angels by day and night and say that they could never live without them, so much do they help them in very many ways.

Among the phenomena of God's presence I would also like to include the singing in tongues that is practised in the Charismatic Renewal. At the beginning of Christianity, this was seen as the very sign of the presence of the Holy Spirit. That is clear from the account of the baptism of the first Christians by the apostle Peter as it is given in Chapter Ten of the Acts of the Apostles. The great Pentecostalist David du Plessis maintained that it was a basic phenomenon, and in a way, the least of the charisms. It is, however, very widespread. But he also observed that in those conditions it was not difficult to obtain and that one could have it from an early stage. I quite agree with this point of view. The gift of tongues is a very simple gift of God, who makes one sing like a child, in abandonment and confidence. I think that it uses human psychology in a very simple way, but that God is entirely present in it.

As well as these phenomena of God's presence, there are also the words that God addresses to us personally.

THE WORDS OF GOD

God speaks through human intelligence
God speaks in very different ways. First, he perfects the human intelligence if it is open to his Spirit. He does not use 'direct' ways unless this is necessary. Mostly he helps people to acquire the virtues needed for discernment. We have already mentioned these. Then he sends the gifts of the Holy Spirit, which are not substitutes for the effort of acquiring information and hard thinking, but which work within us and with us. He also helps us to find the good counsellors who can contribute to our en-

lightenment. Equally, he helps us discover good books, if they are needed, and even, at times, makes us hit immediately on the right passages of those books. I have often seen that, especially with *The Imitation of Christ*. It sometimes happens that God galvanises the intelligence, with a precision and an energy that is absolutely astonishing.

To give some examples: a spiritual writer has to produce a book dealing with a holy person. The work is important and can be of advantage to the church. But he has little time. He asks the Holy Spirit to help him and even to act within his intelligence. A first sign is given to him when, in a completely providential way, he discovers documentation that is exactly what is needed for his purpose. Then he starts work. While he needs sleep, he is woken up during the night and, having thus some unoccupied time, he works without fatigue. He has a metre-high mass of documentation on his desk, but every time he needs a document he finds it at once and loses no time. Everything comes together to show that the texts are good ones. The book is finally published and benefits many people. God has spoken and acted through an intelligence in which he dwells.

A medical student has begun her studies; she is deeply converted, and wishes to serve the Lord and people. She has to pass an examination that will be decisive for her. But she is timid in her way of acting and the test is very selective. While waiting her turn she prays. The Lord reveals to her the questions that are going to come up: they are among those she has studied in her exhaustive preparation. But now she has time to remember them without difficulty. When she comes before the board, she can answer what she knows without fear, and she passes. Later, she has a fine career, still in close union with God.

For all that, God does not like people who are lazy, that is 'lukewarm' people. He does not do their work for them. God speaks, and does not leave people in the dark, but he speaks to those who make the effort to hear him.

American charismatics – an actual incident
At the start of the Charismatic Renewal in the United States,

> some charismatics set out in a car to go somewhere. The car broke down. They gathered around it and began asking God to have it repaired. One of them had a word of prophecy from Jesus: 'I learned to be a carpenter, not a mechanic!' So they went straight off to look for a garage![9]

God speaks through the Bible
God also speaks in the Bible. He does so, first, in a general way, because the Bible is a message addressed to everybody. But he also speaks in a precise way to people in particular circumstances. The word of God is not a dictionary to be consulted, but nevertheless it is alive. For this reason God is able to reach the heart of every person through it.

This was well known at the beginning of Christianity. St Augustine was converted as the result of a word of God that was addressed to him from the letters of St Paul, and his friend Alypius was later touched by the same letter. The Franciscans were founded because St Francis three times received connected texts regarding poverty. Later, at the end of his life, he asked Brother Leo to open the Word of God three times again, and he received three connected texts showing him that he would finish his days in a state of conformity with Jesus on the cross, with the stigmata. St Thérèse of the Child Jesus similarly found her personal call in a text from St Paul that touched her very deeply.

That is actually what happens: at a given moment, the distance between the Bible and me partially disappears. God speaks to me directly, I am touched, I know that it is for me, I receive something decisive for myself. In the Charismatic Renewal, where this appeal to the Word of God is widely practised, thousands of examples could be given.

Often such texts are for encouragement. I have read them very many times before, but now, they reach my very heart. Texts like 'You are my well beloved child', or 'I have carved you on the palm of my hands' can one day transform life, when I see that God is addressing them directly and undeniably to me. A group of priests who needed strength one day received while they were praying the words from 2 Cor 4:1: 'Therefore, since it is by God's mercy that we are engaged in this ministry, we do not lose heart.'

Sometimes the Bible texts 'received' are reproaches. Thus a person who has committed some offence 'receives' a text that asks him to look God in the eye. He then finds himself ashamed to do so, and the sin, whose reality he had denied, becomes clear to him. The impact of this brings about his conversion.

At other times, Bible texts can be aids to discernment. There are amusing examples. A Parisian couple had the choice, owing to the husband's job, of moving either to Rennes or Poitiers. They prayed together for discernment because they could not make up their minds. The husband asked the Lord for a text. His wife objected, 'Do you think the Bible says anything about Poitiers or Rennes?' But then the husband 'received' the text where St Paul says that he is going to take the road for Spain. (Rom 15:24) Now, from Paris, the road to Spain passes through Poitiers. So that was where they moved. A more serious example is this: a man was deeply embarrassed because one of his friends had been accused of something very serious. The evidence seemed to tell against his friend, and the man was asked to take up a position that might damage both his friendship and his position in society. At first he was tempted to do so, but then, on reflection, he told himself that there was a chance the accusation might be false. He prayed, opened his Bible, and came on the words: 'Go find your friend: perhaps he has done nothing, and if he has done something, he will not start again.' (Sir 19:13) So he took up a more neutral approach, which allowed him to contact his friend again and, as it turned out, the man was actually innocent. All this brought about the solution of the problem. Had God not stopped him, the outcome might have been tragic.

Naturally, in this case as elsewhere, there is no excuse for failing to use one's common sense. It would be highly unintelligent to use the Bible as a substitute for intelligence. But the Bible and prayer can facilitate intelligence, when God wants that to happen. It is all a matter of the divine goodness and wisdom.

God speaks directly in words

It can also happen that God speaks directly to someone. This can be in different ways. More usually the Lord uses images and interior words. Cases of visual apparitions and words heard with the ear are, in my view, very rare. Still, there are many other manifestations of words of God for people.

God can directly address an interior word to someone. The ear does not hear it, but the person still receives it. It could take the form of an intuition. The mind is absorbed by something a person feels, but which is difficult to express. What allows expression to come is an exterior circumstance that will force us to speak. Thus an event, a question, or sometimes, especially in a prayer group, a direct confrontation: 'You feel something, say it.' This is often what happens with prophecies in prayer meetings. One person has a charism of prophecy (a word addressed in the name of God to a meeting), and another person has a charism of discernment that prompts the first person to speak. For example, in a charismatic community, there were no 'words of knowledge' (in which it is declared that such or such a person is cured of this or that, or is called by God to conversion on one point or another). Some members of the community were praying for one. Then at a particular prayer meeting, someone 'received' the certainty that another person present had been healed of a serious dental condition, but dared not say so. His neighbour turned to him and said, 'You have a word of knowledge. What is it?' He told him, and the word was confirmed.

Sometimes, this word of God is like a memory. Something fixes itself in the memory that was not there before. One day someone asked the Curé d'Ars how he could tell his penitents precise facts about themselves that they had not told him. He found himself saying that it was in him like remembering, like something familiar coming back to him. It seems relatively common for God to act in this way, especially regarding words of knowledge.

At other times, the word is addressed strongly to the person, directly into the intelligence. There is no sound, but it is received by the intelligence exactly as if it had been heard. The word touches the intelligence in a very precise way. There are very many examples. The words can at times come from Mary or other saints. One particular man had gone through a very painful spell, and felt himself to be on the wrong track. He went on a pilgrimage to Notre-Dame de La Salette. Before the statue of the Virgin of the apparition, he 'heard' Mary saying to him: 'But you know well that I love you.' What proved the reality of this word was that grace touched him and converted him at once. With that his difficulties ceased. Again, a young man, who was independent and had a good job, one day received the word: 'Obey your mother.' He was completely surprised but, a few days later, his mother gave him some pieces of good advice, partly on the practical level, which in due course made his life easier.

Sometimes God gives 'interior motions': here it is a question of a word accompanied by something to do, whether a precise action, or a prayer. The motion, as the name indicates, sets a person in movement, in some particular direction. God says, 'Do this', you do it, then afterwards you see the good results.

Two examples of interior motions
A prayer for a priest
A young girl who had a strong spiritual life 'received' interiorly one day the motion to pray for a particular priest. She took note of the day when it happened, and from that moment, prayed faithfully for him. Several years later, she 'received' interiorly the first name of this priest. Later again, she met him and 'recognised' him. She learned his story: he had been living a by no means Christian life, but felt himself converted suddenly and received the call to the priesthood several years before, on the precise day when God had asked the girl to pray for him.

Story of a birth
'It was during the second world war. My husband was a prisoner in a prisoner-of-war camp in Germany, and there was

no reason to think he would be able to return for a long time. I had obtained a permit for a journey, and I made a stop of some hours in Toulouse. There I had the desire to go up to the Basilica of Our Lady of the Bream, where I prayed especially to the Virgin while waiting for my three eldest.

'I was plunged in deep prayer of thanksgiving for these lovely children which I owed to her intercession. Suddenly, I had this unforeseeable and spontaneous prayer: "And now, O Mary, give me another child before the end of the year."

'It was Tuesday 20th February 1941, at 11 o'clock.

'I finished my journey towards Avignon, where we were lodging with my mother-in-law. There I collected some civilian clothes, 'in case my husband returns' and went home. It was Tuesday 27th February.

'On the night of the 27th or 28th I was awakened by a shower of pebbles at my shutter. Trembling I opened the door ... and there I stood before my husband!

'He was as bewildered as I was, and said to me: "I am not coming back to stay, there was no plan for me to take part in an escape from the camp, but I was called upon to do so on Tuesday 20th at 11 o'clock."

'Nine months later, André arrived in the world.'

God speaks directly in images
Quite often, God also uses the way of interior images. In them one sees something, whether confusedly or clearly. It could be a text that can be clearly read, a landscape, a face, or something else. At the same time, a general interpretation is given, but sometimes it is someone else who gets it.

For instance, a priest one day, during a retreat, 'saw' a palm-tree. This surprised him, and after some hesitation, he decided to mention it. Nobody reacted at the time, but at the end of the meeting someone came to see him, in a state of amazement, and explained that this image had a precise sense for him and would enable him to avoid several serious mistakes. At times the images have a strong spiritual sense. I have known people who 'saw' themselves interiorly as it were in the Heart of the Father, or in the arms of Mary. These images corresponded in fact to a true spiritual state, which could not be expressed in words, but which was shown in images given by God.

There are also less 'imaginative' images, more abstract, but for all that significant. A man who had experienced a period of interior trials wondered how it was between him and God, and no longer felt sure of being really his friend. He prayed for the knowledge of how he really was for Christ. One day, in a flash, he 'saw' the depth of his soul, in an 'abstract' image, so to say. It showed the presence of Jesus in the depth of his soul like a brother and a friend, and the man could no longer have any doubt. This re-established his spiritual equilibrium.

Night-visions
Images sometimes take the form of night-visions *(songes)*, which are completely different from dreams *(rêves)*. A dream is subjective, comes from the unconscious, and has a vague and obscure side to it. A night-vision has on the contrary perfect clarity, does not at all trouble the sleep, and has the character of reality. On awakening, it can be completely recalled without effort. It makes its presence felt. It is accompanied by the idea of something to do, and the inclination to do it. It is essentially an interior motion that uses images. There are numerous examples in the Bible, including the gospels and the Acts of the Apostles. I have seen God continuing to speak in this way today.

Some examples of night-visions
St Joseph
Now the birth of Jesus the Messiah took place in this way. When his mother Mary had been engaged to Joseph, but before they lived together, she was found to be with child from the Holy Spirit. Her husband Joseph, being a righteous man, and unwilling to expose her to public disgrace, planned to dismiss her quietly. But just when he had resolved to do this, an angel of the Lord appeared to him in a dream and said,

'Joseph, son of David, do not be afraid to take Mary as your wife, for the child conceived in her is from the Holy Spirit. She will bear a son, and you are to name him Jesus, for he will save his people from their sins.' [...] When Joseph woke from sleep, he did as the angel of the Lord had commanded him; he took her as his wife. (Mt 1:18-24)

St Paul
During the night Paul had a vision: there stood a man of Macedonia pleading with him and saying, 'Come over to Macedonia and help us.' When he had seen the vision, we immediately tried to cross over to Macedonia, being convinced that God had called us to proclaim the good news to them. (Acts 16:9-11)

A religious vocation
A young girl, a student of physical education, who was a Christian, was thinking of building her life on marriage. One night, she had a vision. A religious appeared to her, with a habit she did not know. She was in a very precise garden; it had a statue of the Virgin which she saw clearly. And a voice said to her, 'This religious is you.' She said, 'No!' The same vision came back again a little afterwards, in exactly the same way, and again she replied, 'No!', though less strongly. A third time the vision appeared, and then she said, 'Yes.'

When she awoke, the young girl understood that it was God calling her. She accepted, left her studies, and entered Carmel. All went well but, at the moment of pronouncing her vows, she fell ill. She had to leave the monastery. After recovering, she did not abandon her desire for religious life. She went to visit a Visitation monastery, where the rule is less demanding. There she was surprised to find that the religious wore exactly the habit of the nun in her vision, which she had never seen before. She was brought to the garden: it was exactly the garden of her vision. At the end of the garden path, there was statue of the Virgin bound up with the entire history of the monastery: it was the statue in her vision!

She entered the Visitation convent where she subsequently played an important role.

Spiritual phenomena in daily life
The authenticity of spiritual phenomena is proved by daily life. Cardinal Eyt, a former archbishop of Bordeaux, used to say: 'God is in the details'. He meant the details of life. Part of mystical life is growth in charity and humility. Both of these find their expression in daily reality.

So spiritual phenomena are not valuable 'in themselves'. They have a part to play in the building up of the soul of the one who receives them and in the building up of the church in general. Life in God does not take us out of the universe and does not ask us to abandon human relationships. People who distance themselves from life, whatever their vocation, are faced with a problem. One of my friends is always saying, 'The mystical life begins with the feet.' With greater authority, the philosopher Henri Bergson wrote: 'Mysticism in its complete form is [...] that of the great Christian mystics. [...] There is [in them] an intellectual wholesomeness that is solidly established, exceptional, and easily recognised. It shows itself in a taste for action, in the capacity to adapt oneself and re-adapt oneself to circumstances, in firmness joined to flexibility, in prophetic discernment of what is and what is not possible, in a spirit of simplicity that triumphs over complications, and finally in a high degree of common sense.'[10] That is perfectly true.

*

As people advance in the interior life, they become more at ease regarding spiritual phenomena. They no longer ask for them – if they ever did – and neither do they fear them. It is all a matter of the freedom that God has given to his children. Provided we live with him and he lives in our souls, all is well.

Conclusion

One of the finest aspects of the life of the church at the end of the twentieth and the start of the twenty-first century is her insistence on the call to holiness. The Second Vatican Council affirmed that all Christians are called to holiness: 'All Christ's faithful, whatever their state or their rank, are called to the fullness of the Christian life and the perfection of charity.'[1] Pope John Paul II repeated frequently: 'If baptism truly brings one into the holiness of God by joining us to Christ and dwelling in us by his Spirit, it would be nonsense to be satisfied with a mediocre life, lived under the sign of a minimalist ethic and a superficial religiosity. Asking a catechumen, "Do you want to be baptised?" is at the same time asking him or her, "Do you want to be a saint?" That means pointing out the radical character of the Sermon on the Mount: "Be perfect, as your heavenly Father is perfect".' (Mt 5:48)[2]

This holiness is not the preserve of specialists: 'As the Council itself has explained, it is not to be imagined that this ideal of perfection supposes an extraordinary life that only some 'geniuses' of holiness could practise. The ways of holiness are manifold, and adapted to the vocation of everyone.'[3]

Everyone is called to the interior life, to life with God on this earth, to full self-realisation and to success. That is what God himself wants. Why should anyone delay before setting out on this road? Why drag one's feet if one is already on it? Why not

---

1. Constitution *Lumen Gentium*, n 40.
2. John Paul II, Apostolic Letter *Novo Millenio Ineunte*, n 31.
3. *ibidem*.

sing, together with the heavenly world and all those who love God, a song of praise and glory to the Trinity?

> *Psalm 150*
> Praise God in his holy place,
> Praise him in his mighty heavens.
> Praise him for his powerful deeds,
> Praise his surpassing greatness.
> O praise him with sound of trumpet,
> Praise him with lute and harp.
> Praise him with timbrel and dance,
> Praise him with strings and pipes.
> O praise him with resounding cymbals,
> Praise him with clashing of cymbals.
> Let everything that lives and that breathes,
> Give praise to the Lord.

Notes

CHAPTER ONE
1. Gideon was a warrior-chief whom the Lord sent against more powerful enemies. Because he was afraid, he put God to the test, and laid out a fleece on the ground during the night. He asked God for the fleece to be drenched while the ground remained dry, which is what happened. The next night he made the opposite request, and was thus convinced that God was with him. (See Judges 6:36-40). The fleece is a symbol of the human soul.
2. *En ta présence le soir,* Paris, Saint-Paul, 1986, p 82.
3. Jean Galot, *L'Esprit d'amour,* Paris Desclée de Brouwer, 1959, p 44.
4. Francois Varillon, *L'Humilité de Dieu,* Paris, Le Centurion, 1974, p 107.
5. Augustin Guillerand, *Au seuil de l'abîme,* Paris, Ed. du Cerf-Nouvelle Cité, 1953, p 53.
6. The founder of the work known as L'Arche, to help handicapped people find a worthy and satisfying human and Christian life.
7. Jean Vanier, *La Source des Larmes,* Paris, Parole et Silence, 2001, p 53.
8. 1647-1690. Between 1673 and 1675 she had the apparitions of Christ which showed his heart filled with love for people. This was the origin of the cult of the heart of Jesus in the church, that is, the cult of the love of God given completely for the human race.
9. 1905-1938. She continued the mission of St Margaret Mary by receiving messages from Christ about his mercy for men and women and especially for sinners.
10. Léon Bloy, quoted by Henri de Lubac, *Paradoxes,* Paris, Seuil, 1959, p 47.
11. Jean Vanier, *op. cit.,* p 57.
12. On the point of mediations, may I refer to my book *Peut-on rencontrer Dieu?* [Can one meet God?], Paris, Ed. de L'Emmanuel, 2001, to which this is something of a sequel.
13. 'God is faithful: by him you were called into the fellowship of his Son, Jesus Christ our Lord.' (1 Cor 1:9)

CHAPTER TWO
1. See chapters 6 to 9 of the Book of Wisdom.
2. Romano Guardini, *The Lord,* (French ed.) Paris, 1945,vol 1, p 306 .
3. *Christ in his mysteries,* French original, Maredsous 1919, p 72.
4. Saint Thérèse of the Child Jesus, Manuscript B, 5v°, in *Oeuvres Complètes,* Paris, Ed du Cerf-DDB, 1992.

5. Fr Thomas Philippe, co-founder of l'Arche with Jean Vanier, relying on his own experience and on the work of Thompson, a disciple of Freud who became a Christian, has explained that the first awareness of the tiny child is of love, before becoming animated by an instinct of life or of death. This awareness of love is as it were the central core of our person, one to which are grafted, one by one, the various other forms of awareness. This is why the human person is constituted by love and cannot develop fully without a certain contact with the state of spiritual childhood. See, Thomas Philippe, *Les âges de la vie, I: L'enfance*, 3rd ed.,Troisly Breuil, Les Chemins de l'Arche-La Ferme, 1996.

6. Dr.Archibald D. Hart, *Unmasking Male Depression*, Word Publications, 2001.

7. Henri Boulad, *L'Amour de Dieu*, Sillery (Quebec), Anne Sigier, 2001, p 86.

8. Pierre Daninos, *Les Carnets du major Thompson*, Paris, Hachette, 1954.

9. St Peter compares us to 'new-born' children. (1 Pet 2:2).

10. Jean Vanier, *op. cit.* p 131.

11. The idea of presenting the structure of the human personality under the form of concentric zones, of which the body is the periphery, is due, it seems to Fr H. Caffarel. See H. Carrarel, *Cinq soirées sur la prière intérieure*, Paris, Ed. Feu nouveau, 1980. The presentation is linked with that of the Viennese psychiatrist Victor Frankl who, confronted with a psychoanalytic theory that tended to reduce the human person to a set of impulses, (an 'id'), underlines the central role of the free and responsible 'I'. The theory has been set out by Dr Martine Catta in the context of the Emmanuel Community, of which she is the co-founder. On all these points, see Denis Biju-Duval, *Le Psychique et le Spirituel*, Paris, Ed. De l'Emmanuel, 2001.

12. Gary Chapman, Les Langues de l'Amor. Actions that say: 'I Love You.' Marne-la-Vallée, Ed. Farel, 2002, p 97.

CHAPTER THREE

1. Louis Bouyer, *Introduction à la vie spirituelle*, Paris-Tournai, Desclée et Cie, 1960, p 245.

2. *The Interior Castle*, tr. Peers, Sheed & Ward, London, 1974, p 10.

3. See Jean-Charles Nault, *La saveur de Dieu*, Rome, Lateran University Press, 2002.

4. A sixth-century monk.

5. [It is my belief that many people today deliberately choose a life in which they can prove themselves by means of genuine human values, such as hard work, success in what they undertake, good relations with husband, wife or partner, and with their children, without finding that those who speak to them about God have much to offer in connection with these things. Those who speak of God seem to be at fault in this respect. The religion Jesus taught in the gospels opposed in exactly the same way the religion of his time. This means that evangelisation con-

sists largely in showing how religion supports and consolidates peoples' human values, and deepens them in a way people can appreciate. *Tr.*]
6. St Teresa of Avila, *op. cit.*, p 13.
7. *op. cit.*, p 16.
8. A charism is a special gift of the Holy Spirit for the service of others. See below, p 45.
9. The extreme example is Judas.
10. St Teresa of Avila, *op. cit.*, p 14.
11. We should underline here especially the importance of the sacrament of reconciliation which permits the grace of God to work within us. Frequent confession facilitates to an amazing extent the growth of the spiritual life.
12. The most celebrated commentary on the virtues has always been that of St Thomas Aquinas, in his *Summa Theologiae*, II-IIae ('the second part of the second part').
13. [The author's insistence that such groups be church groups is important. Groups that are not subject to public or official scrutiny can be injurious to the members, as in the case of certain sects and extremist organisations. *Tr.*]
14. St Teresa of Avila, *op. cit.*, p 21.
15. ibid.
16. St Teresa of Avila, *The Way of Perfection*.
17. St Teresa of Avila, *The Interior Castle*, p 21.
18. 'I have known a few souls who have reached this state – I think I might even say a great many, and who, as far as we can see, have lived for many years an upright and carefully ordered life, both in soul and body; and then after all these years, when it has seemed as if they must have gained the mastery over the world, or at least must be completely detached from it, His Majesty has sent them tests which would have been by no means exacting and they have become so restless and depressed in spirit that they have exasperated me. It is of no use offering them advice, for they have been practising virtue for so long as they think they are capable of teaching others and have ample justification for feeling as they do .... It is useless to argue with them, for they brood over their woes and make up their minds that they are suffering for God's sake, and thus never totally understand that it is all due to their own imperfection.' St Teresa of Avila, *op.cit.*, p 24.

CHAPTER FOUR

1. The Congregation for the Doctrine of the Faith, *Some aspects of Chrisitian Meditation*, 15 October 1989, nn 27f.
2. [That it does so is a sign that it is really the Holy Spirit at work. *Tr.*]
3. *The Interior Castle*, p 33.
4. *op. cit.*, p. 38f [with slight adaptations to accommodate the French version used by the author. *Tr.*]

5. [A formula used by the Young Christian Workers movement. *Tr.*]
6. *op. cit.*, p 36f.
7. *op. cit.*, p 34f.
8. *op. cit.*, p 48.

CHAPTER FIVE

1. It must be recognised however that in human life espousal and marriage are the beginning of a journey, while in the spiritual life they are linked with its maturity.
2. This is a form of mysticism that uses the analogy with marriage to speak of the union of the human being with God. See *Dictionnaire de spiritualité*, Paris,Beauchesne, vol 10, 1977, coll 388-408.
3. A woman will readily define herself as a 'spouse' of Christ, but a man might prefer to call himself 'the friend of the bridegroom', in the expression of St John the Baptist. In any case the words 'engagement' and 'marriage' do not have the same resonance for a man. Apart from which, especially at the present time, anything that distances itself from masculinity is shocking for certain men, and legitimately so, I believe.
4. My opinion does not amount to a negative judgement of the classical terminology, and I would understand why some people might prefer to continue using it. Still, I would not wish to hide my difficulties and reservations on the point.
5. Jean-Claud Sagne, *Viens vers le Père. L'enfance spirituelle, chemin de guérison*, Paris, Éd. de l'Emmanuel, 1998.
6. *Amour et silence,* par un Chartreux, Paris, Éd. du Seuil, 1951, p 81f.
7. M.-M. Philippon OP, *La doctrine spirituelle de soeur Élizabeth de la Trinité*, Paris, DDB, 14th ed, 1954.
8. See Eph 2:19.
9. Elizabeth of the Trinity, *Complete Works*, Washington ICS Publications, Vol 1, 1984, p 183f.
10. Col.3:9-11
11. In the sense of carrying out the required prayers and offices, but not in the sense of becoming a song of praise to the glory of God in the way spoken of earlier.
12. Quoted in J. Fernandez de Retana Arostegui, *Entrer dans la contemplation*, Paris, Éd. de l'Emmanuel, 1995, 1st ed., p 230f, 2nd ed., p 158f.
13. On this point , read St John of the Cross, *The Dark Night*, and the commentaries by Marie-Eugène de l'Enfant Jésus, *Je veux voir Dieu*, Venasque, Ed du Carmel, 1988, and Edith Stein (St Teresa Benedicta of the Cross) *The Science of the Cross*, Louvain-Paris, Nauwelaerts, 1957.
14. 'This divine irruption produces a veritable psychological revolution. Intelligence and will up to this acted according to the laws of human action, that is, were guided by their proper object as presented by the senses or other faculties. But now they are subject to the movement of God who comes to them from the depth of the soul ...' Marie Eugène de l'Enfant Jesus, *op. cit.*, pp 756-820.

15. *Amour et silence, op. cit.*, pp 92, 106, 109.
16. See also Dom Anselm Grün, *Apprendre à faire silence*, Paris, DDB, 2001.

CHAPTER SIX

1. Jean Monbourquette, *À chacun sa mission*, Paris, Bayard, 2001, p21. cf Victor Frankl, *Man's Search for Meaning*, NY, Simon and Schuster, 1984.
2. Jean Laplace, *Preparing for Spiritual Direction*, Chicago, Franciscan Herald Press, 1975, pp 23ff.
3. André Louf, *La grace peut davantage. L'accompagnment spirituel*, Paris, DDB, 1992, pp 17-20.
4. *op. cit.*, 1st ed, p 211, 2nd ed., p 142.
5. Bernard Peyrous, *Le Père Noailles. Un prophète pour aujourd'hui*, Paris, Éd Saint-Paul, 2001.
6. Hervé-Marie Catta and Bernard Peyrous, *Le Feu et l'Espérance. Pierre Goursat, fondateur de la Communauté de l'Emmanuel*, Paris, Éd. de l'Emmanuel, 1994.
7. 'Marthe Robin, 1902-2002', in *l'Alouette, Revue des Foyers de Charité*, n 210, avril 2002.
8. The *Foyers de Charité* are devoted mainly to the spiritual formation of lay-people by means of retreats.
9. At the present time, 2005, there are some 70 *Foyers*, in Europe, Africa, America and Asia. Her cause for beatification is quite advanced, with our author as its Postulator. *Tr.*

CHAPTER SEVEN

1. Bl William Chaminade (1761-1850) founded Marian communities specialising in education at Bordeaux, in France. He was beatified in 2000. *Tr.*
2. This section replaces one on The French School of Spirituality in the original. *Tr.*
3. J.-C. Darrigaud, *Tout soif a son eau. Chiara Lubich et les Focolari*, Paris, Nouvelle Citré, 1978; M. Pochet, *Dialogue avec Chiara Lubich*, Paris, Nouvelle Cité, 1983; *l movimento dei Focolari*, Rome, Città Nuova, 1986; Jim Gallagher, *Chiara Lubich, Dialogo e profezia*, Cinisello Balsamo (Milano), San Paolo,1999.18. Lk 24:13-35.
4. Chiara Lubich, *Jésus Eucharistie*, Paris, Nouvelle Cité, 1981, p 61f.
5. J.-C. Darrigaud, *op. cit.*, p 123. See Judith Provilus, *Gesù in mezzo nel peneiero di Chiara Lubich*, Rome, Città Nuova, 1981.
6. Chiara Lubich, *Pourquoi m'as-tu abondonne? Le secret de l'unit'é*, Paris, Nouvelle Cité, 1989, p 10f.
7. Ibid, p 21.
8. See J.-C. Darrigaud, op. cit., p 111.
9. H-M. Catta and B. Peyrous, *Le Feu et l'Espérance*, op. cit.
10. Albert-Marie de Monléón, *Rendez témoimage. Le renouveau charismatique catholique*, preface by Cardinal J.-M. Lustiger, Paris, Mame, 1998.

11. *Coutumier de la Communouté de l'Emmanuel, pro manuscripto*, 2nd ed., 2002, p 10.
12. 'The Virgin will conceive and bring forth a son who shall be called Emmanuel.' (Is 7:14 and Mt 1:23) In the name 'Emmanuel', God with us, the whole vocation of the community is summed up. It is to bring salvation to people that Christ-Emmanuel has come into the world, approached us, incarnated himself. For the members of the Community, 'to be Emmanuel' in the image of Christ means living union with God in the world, becoming apostles and witnesses of mercy, agreeing to live a simple life in the spirit of poverty, giving Mary a place in their life.' (*Ibid.*, Preamble, p 7)
13. Ibid., p 12.
14. Decree of approbation of the Statutes, 8 December 1992.
15. See, *Sainte Marguerite-Marie et le message de Paray-le-Monial*, Paris, Desclée, 1993; *Le Coeur du Christ pour un monde nouveau, op. cit.*; *Pour une civilisation du Coeur. Vers la glaciation or le réchauffement du monde?* Paris, Éd. de l'Emmanuel, 2000.

CHAPTER EIGHT

1. St Teresa of Avila, *Autobiography*, chap 11.
2. Here are two important works on the point: Thomas Philippe, *The plans of God's love for humankind*, Trosly-Breuil, Les Chemins de l'Arche, 2nd ed, 1986; *Vers la maturité spirituelle*, by a Carthusian monk, Paris, Presses de la Renaissance, 2002.
3. J.Voillaume, *Lettres aux Fraternités, I. Temoins silencieu de l'amitié divine*, Paris, 3rd ed, 1960.
4. See also Jacques Gauthier, *La crise de la quarantaine*, Paris, Le Sarment-Fayard, 2000.
5. The subjects of the religious vows of chastity, poverty and obedience.
6. The word 'illusion' should not be taken in the sense of the consequence of a mistake, or weak thinking. It is a matter of God revealing things gradually which we could not bear if they were told to us all at once.
7. Quoted by Dom Anselm Grün, *op. cit.,* p 11.
8. J. Voillaume, *op.cit.*, p 16f.
9. Quoted by Dom Anselm Grün, *op. cit.*, p 14.
10. Dom Anselm Grün, *op.c it.*, p 21.
11. J. Voillaume, *op. cit.*, p 22f.
12. We find them again in St Paul, Col 3:1-3: 'So if you have been raised with Christ, seek the things that are above, where Christ is seated at the right hand of God. Set your minds on things that are above, not on things that are on earth. For you have died, and your life is hidden with Christ in God.'
13. Quoted by Dom Anselm Grün, *op.cit.*, p 51.
14. Henri J. M. Nouwen, *Lettre à un ami sur la vie spirituelle*, Ville Mont-Royale, Novalis; Paris, Éd du Cerf, 1997, p 98.

CHAPTER NINE

1. Daniel-Ange, *Les blessures que guérit l'amour*, Paris, Pneumathèque, 1979; Pascal Ide, *Connaître ses blessures*, Paris, Éd de l'Emannuel, 1993; Simone Pacot, *L'évangelisation des profoundeurs*, Paris, Éd du Cerf, 2002; Philippe Madre, *La blessure de la vie*, Éd des Béatitudes, 2001.
2. Jean Vanier, *Toute personne est un histoire sacrée*, Paris, Plon, 1994.
3. Simone Pacot, *op. cit.*; Jean Monbourquette, *op. cit.*, pp 71-81.
4. Dr Ross Campbell, *Les enfants en colère. Comprendre une dynamism méconnue*, Richmond (Quebec), 1995.; and, *L'adolescent. Le défi de l'amour inconditionnel*, Richmond (Quebec) 7th ed 1995; and, *Comment vraiment aimer votre enfant*, Richmond (Quebec), Orion, 11th ed 1997.
5. Stan Rougier, *Aime et tu vivras*, Paris, Cana, 1990; Richard et Danelle Borgman, *Le coup de grâce*, Paris, Trinité Média Communications, s.d.
6. Jean Lafitte, *Le pardon transfiguré*, Paris, Desclée-Éd de l'Emmanuel, 1995; Jean-Claude Sagne, *Sacrament de la reconciliation et vie spirituelle*, Paris, Éd de l'Emmanuel-Chemin Neuf, 1995.

CHAPTER TEN

1. When I say 'to my mind', I would wish to add that I am not at all alone in my opinion.
2. An amusing example among thousands is found in Alex Ceslas Rzweuski OP, *Á travers l'invisible crystal, confessions d'un Dominican*, Paris, Plon, 1976, p.494f. On false Marian apparitions, see Joachim Bouflet, *Faussaires de Dieu*, Paris, Presses de la Renaissance, 2000. In a general way, the basic book on the discernment of mystical phenomena continues to be, *The Ascent of Mount Carmel* of St John of the Cross.
3. For example: the great book of August Poulain SJ, *Des grâces d'oraison. Traité de théologie mystique*, 10th ed, Paris Beauchesne, 1922; Auguste Saudreau, *L'état mystique. Sa nature, ses phases, les faits extraordinaires de la vie spirituelle*, Paris, Amat – Arras, Brunet – Angers, G. Grassin, Richou, 1921; H. Jaegen, *La vie de grâce mystique*, Paris, Albin Michel, 1982; *La mistica: Fenomenologia e riflessione teologica*, under the direction of Ermanno Ancilli and of Maurozio Paparozzi, Rome, Città Nuova. 1984, 2 vol.; Joachim Bouflet, *Encyclopédie des faits extraordinaires dans la vie mystique*, Paris, Le Jardin des livres, 2 vols, Paris 2001-2002; *Dictionnaire de l'extraordinaire dans le christianisme*, under the direction of Patrick Sbalchiero, Paris, Fayard, 2002.
4. René Latourelle, *Miracles de Jésus et théologie du miracle*, Paris, Éd du Cerf; Montréal, Bellarmin, 1986; Dr Patrick Theillier, *Et si on parlait des miracles...*, Paris, Presses de la Renaissance, 2001; Georgio Fedalto, *Le Porte del Cielo. Il cristianesimo e I segni dell'aldilà: apparizioni, visioni, testimony*, Milan, San Paolo, 2002.
5. Bilocation is when a person appears to be in two different places at the same time, sometimes hundreds of kilometers apart.
6. Joachin Pouflet, *Encyclopedie des faits extraordinaires...*, *op. cit.*
7. Conrad de Meester (ed), *Brother Lawrence of the Resurrection, The*

Practice of the Presence of God, Institute of Carmelite Studies, Washington DC.

8. [It is in any case rare for a wise spiritual director to *diagnose* anyone's spiritual condition: it is the person being directed who tells the director what he or she has experienced, while the director helps them to do this as best they can. *Tr.*]

9. Still, I have seen God do amazing things, even regarding cars, but those for whom he did them had done all they could themselves.

10. Henri Bergson, *Les deux sources de la morale et de la religion,* Paris, PUF, p 20-24.